D1548841

PR
610
S5

35053
36447

Sitwell

Aspects of Modern Poetry

ASPECTS OF
MODERN POETRY

ASPECTS OF
MODERN POETRY

BY

EDITH SITWELL

Essay Index Reprint Series

 BOOKS FOR LIBRARIES PRESS
FREEPORT, NEW YORK

First Published 1934
Reprinted 1970

INTERNATIONAL STANDARD BOOK NUMBER:
0-8369-1684-0

LIBRARY OF CONGRESS CATALOG CARD NUMBER:
74-117845

PRINTED IN THE UNITED STATES OF AMERICA
BY
NEW WORLD BOOK MANUFACTURING CO., INC.
HALLANDALE, FLORIDA 33009

PR
610
S5

36447

To
HELEN ROOTHAM

CONTENTS

NOTE TO ORIGINAL EDITION

THIS book is in no way intended as a complete survey of modern poetry. It deals only with some significant phases. I hope, later, to produce a second volume in which I shall discuss the poetry of Sir Henry Newbolt, Sir J. C. Squire, Messrs. Walter de la Mare, Sturge Moore, A. E., Edmund Blunden and Siegfried Sassoon.

I have to thank the authors for permission to reprint the poems which appear in this volume, and also the Editor of the *Morning Post* for allowing me to reprint part of the first chapter of this book.

E. S.

CHAPTER I

PASTORS AND MASTERS

" WE do not," said Warton in his Essay on Pope, "sufficiently attend to the difference there is between a man of wit, a man of sense, and a true poet. . . . Which of these characters is the most valuable and useful, is entirely out of the question: all I plead for, is, to have their several provinces kept distinct from each other; and to impress on the reader that a clear head, and acute understanding, are not sufficient, alone, to make a poet ; that the most solid observations on human life, expressed with the utmost elegance and brevity, are morality, and not poetry."

It is from an exuberance of this morality, perverted or unperverted, that much of the newest poetry suffers in this age, and it is a morality which is rarely expressed with elegance and brevity, and seldom arises from a clear head and acute understanding.

The decay of taste in this age is due, in part, to the fact that the public mind is still overshadowed by those Aberdeen granite tombs and monuments, the classical scholars of Victorian times. The public had a restless feeling that it disliked being bored. But it had not yet assimilated the fact that there is more than one kind of bore. The worst, had the public known it, was still to come.

A period of lifelessness often succeeds a great age in poetry; but even in the midst of the great Victorian age we find an undergrowth of extreme debility, of excessively bad minor poetry which took a pride in poverty of expression. The mania for the Dilettante, which has nearly succeeded in ruining the poetry of today, began with the Victorians—together with placid understatements of some personal experience, expressed either in threadbare texture, or in one of an unpleasing muddy thickness. In the Victorian age, too, we find the first dawning of that wish to compare poetry with science, those pathetic attempts to define God and the Good which are at the bottom of most of the bad poetry of today. Indeed, the verse of some of the youngest writers in no way excels Emerson's in point of vigour. There is a difference of sound, inasmuch as the poems of the younger school, technically, are founded on a complete misapprehension of Gerard Manley Hopkins, whereas Emerson's verse is an attempt at a different kind of " Grand manner." In Emerson, there is a general lifeless overstatement, in the newer poets an equally lifeless understatement. Emerson uses bloated, lifeless words; the fault of certain of the younger modern poets is that they use shrunken, bloodless words. Therein lies the only difference; otherwise, bad minor poetry is exactly what bad minor poetry has always been.

It was also in the Victorian age that the desire first arose amongst poets to fit in, practically, with

ordinary everyday occasions, not to transmute these,
but to copy them faithfully. There was a frightened
rush to conform to the point of view of the Man
in the Street, to provide a simple dress for his
simple thoughts, with simple gloves to protect his
hands from the touch of raw life. The threadbare
places in these gloves were always scrupulously
patched ; and who cared if the threads did not
match the fabric in colour, or in texture—if the
patching was now lumpy, now thin ?

We find, in this time, a general outbreak of tea-
table condolences, and tearfulness over the artless
prattle of little children, tendernesses which grew
side by side with the bloodless, nerveless escapes
from life of O'Shaughnessy and Andrew Lang—
poems which already foreshadowed that loss of the
visual sense which is one of the major faults of
modern poetry. These writers have been used by
certain modern critics as an excuse for denying
that the great poets whom they imitated so lifelessly
were great poets. In fact, their worthlessness is at
the root of the present denial that poetry should
be regarded as an art, and not a treatise or a tract,
or a book on economics.

We had, too, Mr. Austin Dobson, and his Marcel
Waves, the wriggling, giggling horrors of his
Triolets and other imitations of French forms :

> " I intended an Ode,
> And it turned to a Sonnet.
> It began *à la mode*,
> I intended an Ode ;
> But Rose crossed the road

> In her latest new bonnet ;
> I intended an Ode ;
> And it turned to a Sonnet."

These served as a contrast to the booming and bursting and bumping and bumptiousness of W. R. Henley, that forerunner of the Boer War, and the tasteful amateurishness (I speak of his verse only) of Robert Louis Stevenson. Sheltering tenderly under the protection of those manly boomings and burstings, we find Mrs. Meynell's limp exhortations to virtue, bearing (to paraphrase a description given by Mr. E. F. Benson of the profile of one of his characters) as much resemblance to the cameos they have been held to resemble as the heads on postage stamps.

Above all, we find pretence of emotion, and not emotion itself, as in the works of that completely lifeless writer, William Johnson Cory, giving himself away in his longing for " sexless souls, ideal quires, unwearied voices, wordless strains." I do not hesitate to say that his worthless poem " Heraclitus " has done as much harm to the unilluminated public taste as has T. E. Brown's patronizing colloquy with God in a Garden.

The persons whom I have mentioned are either poetasters, or versifiers of so insignificant a character that it is hardly worth while to distinguish the features of one from another. It would not, indeed, profit us to mention these, were it not that the average uninstructed reader has, ever since the time of Shelley, Keats, Wordsworth and Coleridge, been led on one wild-goose chase after another.

One of the most noteworthy things about all the versifiers whom I have mentioned is the fact that they had practically no rhythmical impetus whatever (excepting in the case of Austin Dobson, where it resulted only in his catching his toe-nails in his beard) and that the texture of a poem meant nothing to them, either from a melodic point of view, or as a means of lengthening a line or changing the speed. I said in my Life of Pope that his feeling for this most important matter of texture was so phenomenally sensitive that, had the verses been transformed into flowers, he could have told lily from rose, buttercup from cowslip or from primrose, in no matter how moonless and starless a night.

This feeling for texture was lost to the writers of whom I speak. But not only did the texture of a line, the fabric of a poem, mean nothing to them; the shape and weight or lightness of a word, itself as entity, these too were ignored. For these writers, words cast no shadows, had no radiance, were not of varying heights and depths. They did not know that a word can glitter like a star reflected in deep water, can be round and smooth-skinned as an apple.

It may, indeed, be said that with the exception of those great poets, Gerard Manley Hopkins and W. B. Yeats, and with the possible exception of Francis Thompson, the poets writing between the years 1880 and 1900 had little or nothing to recommend them. On the one hand, we had the lifeless if pretty falsities of the unhappy Ernest Dowson, though it cannot be said that these are

entirely false, for occasionally a genuine feeling slips
through. On the other hand, we have what is
claimed to be the perfection of Mr. A. E. Housman's
"Shropshire Lad." I have the greatest respect for
the integrity of Professor Housman, and I am not
intending any discourtesy to him when I say that to
my feeling, the cramped and rheumatic eight-
syllable lines, the threadbare texture in which he
finds, as a rule, his expression, are not suitable to
his themes. Ploughboys never moved so elegantly,
men about to be hanged never expressed their
sentiments with such neatness ; the broken-hearted
groan or they whisper, but they do not confine
their outpourings to the brevity of such epi-
grammatic quatrains as these. In short, life and
death are not like that. Yet, strangely enough, in
Marvell's great poem "To His Coy Mistress,"
T. S. Eliot's great poem "Whispers of Immortality," the vast imagination of these is preserved
within the prim eight-syllable line, and this,
indeed, even heightens the effect in both these
poems, shows us, in its narrow grave, the eternal
skeleton. Wherein lies the difference ? In the
fact that we feel a controlled and terrible passion
underlying Marvell's and Eliot's verses, an explosive
force heaving beneath the surface of the lines.

"The Shropshire Lad" is claimed to be great
poetry because of the bareness of the line, the
absolute lack of decoration. But to my feeling,
that bareness is due as much to lack of vitality as
to anything else. It is certain that the greatest
impressiveness of emotion is gained by an absolute
simplicity. But in Professor Housman's poems one

reader, at least, feels that this simplicity is not invariably the result of passion finding its expression in one inevitable phrase, inhabiting it as the soul inhabits the body, but is sometimes the result of a thin and threadbare texture. This texture is not strong enough to contain an explosive force, or the possibility of a passionate upheaval under the line. The rigidity of the structure does not seem like the rigidity of grief; it seems to arise from stiffness, from an insufficient fluidity. The verse is for the most part rhythmically dead. This is not always the case, however, as we shall see if we read " The Immortal Part."

> " When I meet the morning beam,
>   Or lay me down at night to dream,
>   I hear my bones within me say,
>   Another night, another day.
>
> When shall this slough of sense be cast,
>   This dust of thoughts be laid at last,
>   The man of flesh and soul be slain
>   And the man of bone remain ? "

This is nearly, but not quite, great poetry.

If we read these lines, and the equally admirable poem " Is My Team Ploughing," we shall find in both a control that is impressive ; and the poems are not understated. In both the rigidity is necessary to the theme, and is the rigidity of grief.

Compare " The Immortal Part," however, with these lines from Mr. Eliot's " Whispers of Immortality," and we shall see the difference, admirable as is Professor Housman's poem.

" Donne, I suppose, was such another
Who found no substitute for sense ;
To seize and clutch and penetrate,
Expert beyond experience,

He knew the anguish of the marrow
The ague of the skeleton ;
No contact possible to flesh
Allayed the fever of the bone."

These lines, bare as the immortal skeleton, are,
like Professor Housman's, based on the eight-
syllabled norm ; but Mr. Eliot's have the strength
of the bones, that are no longer held together even
by the cold. They have the undying passion that
has known all experience and has learnt that all
is vain.

I think one reason that Mr. Eliot's lines have this
appalling impressiveness is that the first and third
lines are not rhymed, so that a freezing air creeps
through the gap. Another difference between the
two fragments quoted is that Professor Housman's
lines move faster than Mr. Eliot's, which is always
the case with eight-syllabled lines which are rhymed
A—A, B—B, unless some strength of consonants,
some broadening or deepening or lengthening of
the line brought about by the vowel-scheme,
alters this otherwise inevitable result.

Professor Housman's understatements are rarely
impressive. To my astonishment, I find that
Mr. Charles Williams, a critic who is usually
possessed of great discernment, when speaking of
a poem called " Hell Gate," in a later volume than
" The Shropshire Lad," claims that " Many things

have been said at Hell Gate since Dante and Milton passed there, but few phrases are so satisfying as that of this newcomer : ' To Sin's Smile,' ' Met again, my lass, said I.' "

" It is as great in its way," continues the critic, " as Farinata in his burning tomb."

How can this cramped and trivial phrase be held to be great ? In what way does it increase our experience ? What passion does it express ? What wisdom does it contain ?

But to return to " The Shropshire Lad " ; a spurious pathos, springing, however, from a perfectly genuine feeling, is gained from time to time by the juxtaposition of such themes as cricket and death :

> " See the son of grief at cricket
> Trying to be glad.
>
> .   .   .   .   .
>
> Try I will : no harm in trying.
> Wonder 'tis how little mirth
> Keeps the bones of man from lying
> On the bed of earth."

It is claimed by admirers of cricket and of war that Waterloo was won on the playing fields of Eton. If this may be held to be true, cricket did, on that occasion, bring a great many men to their death. But I do not think that Professor Housman has explained to us clearly enough how it is that cricket has saved men from dying. If he means us to understand that cricket, and cricket alone, has prevented men from committing suicide, then their continuation on this earth seems hardly worth while.

Professor Housman's poems show an obvious delight in country pleasures, but little or no visual sense, or, in any case, no gift for illuminating or transmuting things seen. What, for instance, do the following lines add to our experience :

> " And since to look at things in bloom
> Fifty springs are little room,
> About the woodland I will go
> And see the cherry hung with snow. . . ."

Nothing.

We had now reached an age of literary cricketers, of poets who wore their school colours, and played the game, and addressed members of the same social class as " Man," members of the working class as " Lad."

Mr. Housman was followed by a school of poets, rather loosely held together by their sub-Wordsworthian ideals. To these men rhetoric and formalism were abhorrent, partly, no doubt, because to manage either quality in verse, the writer must have a certain gift for poetry.

In the age of which I speak, we find the first shy buds of those full-flowered transcriptions of Robert Elsmere into blank verse which enliven the pages of a certain monthly arbiter of our taste. In that verse, as in much of the verse of our time, the praise of worthy home life alternated with swollen inflated boomings and roarings about the Soul of Man. These beauties reigned triumphant, together with healthy, manly, but rather raucous shouts for beer, and advertisements of certain rustic parts of England, to the accompaniment of

a general clumsy clodhopping with hob-nailed
boots. Birds became a cult. Any mention of the
nest of a singing-bird threw the community into
a frenzy. Dreary plaster-faced sheep with Alex-
andra fringes and eyes like the eyes of minor German
royalties, limpid, wondering, disapproving, un-
comprehending, these were admired, as were bull-
dogs weeping tears of blood. Nor was Romance
absent. At one moment, any mention of " little
Juliet," " Helen of Troy," or of Troy itself, roused
a passionate interest. The names alone were
sufficient. Again, any allusion to a violin—although
this must always be called a fiddle—any simple
description of a gaffer doddering in the village
alehouse, melted the audience to tears. Yet
with all this romantic simplicity, the business man's
careful logic was never absent, combined, strangely
enough, with the legendary innocence of the
country clergyman (this last trait being a tribute
to the memory of the unfortunate Wordsworth).
Then arose Mr. D. H. Lawrence's practical Jaeger
school of verse. Many things were discovered ;
the only thing that was not discovered was poetry.
At the same time, a school of American-Greek
posturants, resembling not so much marble statues
as a white-tiled bathroom, began to exude a thin
stream of carefully chosen watery words. In
lifelessness, the verses of these persons resembled
those of Ernest Dowson, only they are colder, less
sentimental than Dowson's poems. Added to these
misfortunes, we were then afflicted by the shrill
moronic cacklings of the Surréalistes, laying never
so much as an addled egg.

To these, are now added fresh menaces. Any
mention of any really important Business House
entitles us, at once, to be regarded as poets. No
longer must the Village Idiot confine himself to
his village ; he must gibber round the mouthings
of Fleet Street, ponder over them, reconstruct them.

.   .   .   .   .   .

In the midst of these troubles, most of them
noisy ones, we may find time to wonder at
the number of dilettanti, persons interesting,
no doubt, to the home circle, but unwary
in straying outside that benevolent shelter,
who are now giving their opinions in loud and shrill
voices on the subject of poetry. Egged on by a
small but excited crowd consisting, I imagine, of
admiring aunts and a few infant Ajaxes from the
universities, bent upon defying and being impertinent to their betters, these gentlemen squeak
defiance, and, with the best intentions in the world,
do a great deal of harm to poetry.

The critics in question have a singularly debilitated, semi-puritanical dislike of beauty in poetry,
so that we feel that their love of the art is platonic,
not passionate. They succeed, indeed, when
writing about poetry, in combining the attitude of
a dear old country clergyman preaching a sermon
on the Woman taken in Adultery, with the powers
of expression possessed by those interesting but
amorphous persons who are placed in charge of a
Sultan's female household.

Amongst our pastors and masters, we must place, first and foremost, Dr. F. R. Leavis, a gentleman who plays in the literary life of Mr. T. S. Eliot, and in a lesser degree, in that of Mr. Ezra Pound, much the same part as that played by the faithful Dr. Watson in the life of Sherlock Holmes, listening, wondering, chronicling, bludgeoning the dangerous, and, as a rule, bringing about much the same results as were obtained by Dr. Watson when he was left to himself. Dr. Leavis has not, however, Dr. Watson's bluffness—his strong suit is sensibility. Take, for instance, his comment on Mr. Eliot's note on the significance of Tiresias in " The Waste Land " : (" The two sexes met in Tiresias. What Tiresias sees, in fact, is the substance of the poem.") Dr. Leavis adds, gravely : " A cultivated modern is (or feels himself to be) intimately aware of the experience of the opposite sex."

Well, well !

Dr. Leavis has a transcendental gift, when he is writing sense, for making this appear to be nonsense. On page 13 of his book " New Bearings in English Poetry " we find this very lucid summing-up of the powers that distinguish the poet from his fellow-men. (Elsewhere, on page 89, he confesses that " I have been a good deal embarrassed by the fear of dwelling on the obvious to the extent of insulting the reader.") " Indeed, his (the poet's) capacity for experiencing and his power of communication are indistinguishable, not merely because we should not know of the one without the other, but because his power of making words express what he feels is indistinguishable from his awareness of what he feels. He is unusually sensitive, unusually aware, more sincere and more himself than the ordinary man can be. He knows what he feels and knows what he is interested in."

The above, in its command over the English language and prose rhythms, is matched by the following passage, from the Doctor's essay on Milton's verse (*Scrutiny*, September, 1933). " But the case remained unelaborated, and now that Mr. Eliot has become academically respectable those who refer to *it* show commonly that they cannot understand *it* " (the italics are mine). Are we to gather from this that Mr. Eliot *is* " It," or that Dr. Leavis *has* " It' ' ?

I admire, too, this passage from his essay on Mr. Pound (page 138, " New Bearings "). " In Mauberley . . . the verse is extraordinarily subtle, and its subtlety is the subtlety of the sensibility that it expresses."

Dr. Leavis is very attached to the words " sensibility," " awareness," " cultivation " and " modern consciousness." We are warned, however, on page 93, that " there are ways in which it is possible to be too conscious." He has a genuine, natural and cultivated gift for wincing, and this causes him from time to time, when probing a poem, to use phrases, graciously antiseptic, which remind one of a tenderly-ruthless, white-robed young dentist :

(" And round his head the aureole clings
And he is clothed in white ")—

probing and dressing a decayed molar, discovering

the root of the trouble, and explaining it to the patient :

" A matter of subtle tension within, pressure upon the still smooth curves."
—*Scrutiny*, September, 1933.

" A profound inner disturbance ; a turbid pressure of emotions from below."
—*Scrutiny*, June, 1934.

" In Mauberley we feel a pressure of experience, an impulsion from deep within."
—" New Bearings," page 138.

" What we are looking for is a handling of words that registers a pressure of sensibility."
—*Scrutiny*, June, 1934.

Lives there a man with soul so dead that he cannot smell the disinfectant in these phrases ?

The " adult, sensitive and adequate mind " of which Dr. Leavis is so proud, registers a pathetic if amusing tremor at the thought of being associated in any way with a garden suburb. This is shown in his reference to Rupert Brooke : " He energised the Garden Suburb Ethos with a certain original talent and the vigour of a prolonged adolescence." I cannot refrain from asking myself why these haunts of virtue should be so despised. Perhaps Dr. Leavis has a closer acquaintance with them than I can claim, and has adult sensitive and adequate reasons for this scorn. For nothing can satisfy his ardent spirit. He has even found dis-illusionment in what he calls " a cultivated drawing-room " [*sic*]. " I have heard it announced in a

cultivated drawing-room that the choruses from
Gilbert Murray's ' Euripides ' are some of the
finest poetry in the English language." Here,
indeed, we have both subtlety of thought and of
expression.

Having examined this natural sensitiveness under
our microscope, we will now return to Dr. Leavis'
critical gifts.

There are moments in the writings of this
gentleman when, were we not aware that Dr.
Leavis is *not* Alexander Pope, and that Mr. Eliot
and Mr. Pound in no way resemble Mr. Ambrose
(Namby-Pamby) Phillips, we might believe that
we were reading once again Mr. Pope's understanding praise of Mr. Phillips' Pastorals.

It is, perhaps, Mr. Pound who has inspired
Dr. Leavis to his finest flights ; take, for instance,
this sentence : " However uncongenial one may
find his eclectic æstheticism, his devotion to the
elegance of Circe's hair, it has been accompanied
by intense seriousness. Mr. Pound is not an
American for nothing."

We will now quote (and in this I am following
the example of Mr. John Sparrow in " Sense and
Poetry ") the second division of Mr. Pound's "Mauberley," and then see what Dr. Leavis has to say
about it.

Note.—To do the poem justice it must be quoted whole.

" Qu'est-ce qu'ils savent de l'amour, et
        Qu'est-ce qu'ils peuvent comprendre ?

" S'ils ne comprennent pas la poésie, s'ils ne
sentent pas la musique, qu'est-ce qu'ils peuvent

comprendre de cette passion en comparaison avec
laquelle la rose est grossière et le parfum des
violettes un tonnerre ? "

CAID ALI.

" For three years, diabolus in the scale,
He drank ambrosia,
All passes, ANANGKE prevails,
Came an end, at last, to that Arcadia.

He had moved amid her phantasmagoria,
Amid her galaxies,
NUKTIS'AGALMA.

.   .   .   .   .

Drifted . . . drifted precipitate,
Asking time to be rid of . . .
Of his bewilderment ; to designate
His new-found orchid. . . .

To be certain . . . certain . . .
(Amid aerial flowers) . . . time   for
    arrangements—
Drifted on
To the final estrangement ;

Unable in the supervening blankness
To sift TO AGATHON from the chaff
Until he found his sieve . . .
Ultimately, his seismograph :

Given that is his ' fundamental passion ,'
This urge to convey the relation
Of eyelid and cheekbone
By verbal manifestations ;

To present the series
Of curious heads in medallion—

He had passed, inconscient, full gaze,
The wide-banded irides
And Botticellian sprays implied
In their diastasis ;

Which anæsthesis, noted a year late,
And weighed, revealed his great affect,
(Orchid), mandate
Of Eros, a retrospect.

.   .   .   .   .

Mouths biting empty air,
The still stone dogs,
Caught in metamorphosis, were
Left him as epilogues."

To Dr. Leavis " it seems impertinent to explain
what so incomparably explains itself, and all
elucidation looks crude." . . . " The poem is
poignantly personal, and yet, in its technical perfection, its ironical economy, impersonal and de-
tached. Consider, for instance, the consummate
reserve of this :

' Unable in the supervening blankness
To sift TO AGATHON from the chaff
Until he found his sieve . . .
Ultimately, his seismograph : ' "

" With what subtle force," exclaims the Doctor,
" the shift of image in the last line registers the
realization that the ' orchid ' was something more,
the impact more than æsthetic ! and with what
inevitability the ' seismograph ' and the scientific

terminology and manner of what follows convey
the bitter irony of realization in retrospect."

Now, Mr. Pound is one of the finest living poets,
and can survive the admiration of Dr. Leavis;
but when we read the passage quoted above, it is
impossible not to be reminded of Pope's essay on
the unfortunate Mr. Phillips:

"It is a justice I owe to Mr. Phillips," observed
Mr. Pope, gravely, "to discover those parts in
which no man can compare with him. First, that
beautiful rusticity, of which I shall only produce
two instances out of a hundred not yet quoted:

> ' O woeful day! O day of woe! quoth he;
>   And woeful I, who live the day to see.' "

The simplicity of diction, the melancholy flowing
of the numbers, the solemnity of the sound, and
the easy turn of the words in our dirge (to make
use of our author's expression) are extremely elegant.

In another of his Pastorals, a shepherd utters a
dirge not much inferior to the former, in the
following lines:

> "Ah me the while! ah me, the luckless day,
>   Ah luckless lad! the rather might I say,
>   Ah silly I! more silly than my sheep,
>   Which on the flowery plain I once did keep."

"How he still charms the ear by this artful
repetition of the epithets! and how significant is
the third line. I defy the most common reader to
repeat them without feeling some motions of
compassion."

Dr. Leavis touches nothing that he does not adorn. He is delightful on the subject of Milton, whom he decided to " show up " in his magazine *Scrutiny*.

Dr. Leavis has " scrutinized " Milton, and has decided that there is very little there. The sound of a great deal of Milton, too, affects Dr. Leavis much as the sound of a motor-bicycle affects my less sensitive nervous system. " We find ourselves . . . flinching from the foreseen thud that comes so inevitably, and at last, irresistibly ; for reading ' Paradise Lost ' is a matter of resisting, of standing up against the verse-movement, of subduing it into something tolerably like sensitiveness, and in the end our resistance is worn down, we surrender at last to the inescapable monotony of the ritual." We are warned, however (for he is scrupulously fair) that " a writer of Mr. Allen Tate's repute as critic, poet, and intellectual leader " can see something in the poor old gentleman. But then, having from a sense of justice handed Milton this necessary testimonial we are told that " He exhibits a feeling for words rather than a capacity for feeling through words. . . . The extreme and consistent remoteness of Milton's medium from any English that was ever spoken is an immediately relevant consideration. It became, of course, habitual to him ; but habituation could not sensitize a medium so cut off from speech—speech that belongs to the emotional and sensory texture of actual living and is in resonance with the nervous system ; it could only confirm an impoverishment of sensibility ! "

These lines, proclaims the Doctor, are an
" offence " :

.   .   .   .   .

" Thus was the place,
   A happy rural seat of various view ;
   Groves whose rich trees wept odorous Gummes
      and Balme,
   Others whose fruit burnisht with Golden Rinde
   Hung amiable, Hesperian fables true,
   If true, here onely of delicious taste."

These thunderbolts are followed as usual by a
lot of wincing and whimpering about " sensitiveness " and by an analysis of a certain passage from
Milton. The unfortunate thing about this analysis
is that it transpires that Dr. Leavis does not hear
where the stresses fall ; this is where he places them :

" The hasty multitude
   Ad*mi*ring enter'd, and the wòrk some praise
   And *some* the Architect, his hànd was known
   Where Scepter'd Angels held their rèsidence
   And sat as Princes."

Now, what makes this, apart from the irration-
ality of the stressing, so delightful, is that Dr. Leavis
does not realize that the passage in question is,
comparatively speaking, light in texture, and he has
therefore chosen it as an example of " thudding."
Yet " praise " and " Princes " are the only words
beginning with heavy consonants. If there is any
" thudding " at all it is to be found only in the
p and in the thickness of the m in " multitude "

and " admiring." As for his interpretation of the
stressing, it is sad to see Milton's great lines bobbing
up and down in the sandy desert of Dr. Leavis'
mind with the grace of a fleet of weary camels.

It is only fair to Dr. Leavis to say, however,
that much of his essay on Mr. Eliot's poetry, in
" New Bearings," would prove invaluable to a
reader who is ignorant of the derivations from
which Mr. Eliot has drawn some of his images.
There may, for instance, be readers who do not
know that in Miss J. L. Weston's book " From
Ritual to Romance " the Waste Land has a significance in terms of Fertility Ritual. And as
Dr. Leavis points out, " Vegetation cults, fertility
ritual with their sympathetic magic, represent a
harmony of human culture with the natural enrivon-
ment, and express an extreme sense of the unity
of the life.   In the modern Waste Land

> ' April is the cruellest month, breeding
>   Lilacs out of the dead land,'

and bringing no quickening to the human spirit."

This would, as I have said, prove an invaluable
help to the class of reader to which I have
alluded.

And now we must take our leave of Dr. Leavis,
and turn our attention to the work of another
critic of equal importance, Mr. Geoffrey Grigson.
I hope that it will not offend the aunts and other
admirers of both these gentlemen if I say that the
only difference between them lies in Dr. Leavis'
gift for wincing. Mr. Grigson has not yet, I

believe, taken up this occupation seriously as an indoor sport.

Note.—If I am accused by cultivated gentlewomen of both sexes of discourtesy towards Dr. Leavis, I would remind my readers that he has said of me in his " New Bearings " that I " belong to the history of publicity rather than that of poetry."

It would be idle, perhaps, to speculate as to why a wish for self-advertisement should be shown by the fact of a poet practising his or her art, and why it is *not* self-advertisement when a person who is not a poet publishes his opinion on an art which some might think nature has not fitted him to judge.

Mr. Geoffrey Grigson is not as amusing as Dr. Leavis, but there is still considerable pleasure to be derived from contemplating him.

In an unconsciously extremely funny article in a Sunday newspaper (an article which I discovered, afterwards, had been written by the City Editor) we were told : " There is nothing shrinking about Geoffrey Grigson " (our old friend G. G.). " He is aggressive, eager, dogmatic. Today he will ram down the throat of the assembly the merits of Wyndham Lewis. A few months ago it was some other godling. He enthrones and dethrones."

The thought of Mr. Grigson " enthroning " or " dethroning " Mr. Lewis has caused me a certain amount of amusement, and it is probably no less a source of amusement to Mr. Lewis.

Note.—I feel it my duty to warn Mr. Eliot, whilst contemplating the enthronements in *New Verse*, that if he is not very careful, he will get himself dethroned—if not by Mr. Grigson, by another contributor to *New Verse*, for I find this sinister sentence in a review by Mr. Louis Macniell of Miss Laura Riding's " The Life of the Dead " (*New Verse*, December, 1933), " How refreshing to turn from her sophistication to . . . Mr. Eliot (*however unctuous his romanticism or after-dinner his pedantry*)" (the italics are mine).

Now let us see the kind of verse that is being " enthroned " by Mr. and Mrs. Grigson in *New Verse*. Actually I believe that Mrs. Grigson is the editor of this educational work, but as the husband is responsible for the torts of the wife, he also must be blamed for the clotted nonsense enshrined by her. The City Editor assures us that " somewhere among these names, that are names as yet to a limited world, to a coterie, lurks the name that is to be immortal." Reading their works, I can only murmur, with Mr. George Robey, " Very likely." " Is it," continues the City Editor, " Gavin Ewart ?

> ' The lack of sense can bring
> Certain definite compensations ;
> We cannot read the ironic obituaries
> Tactfully written by our relations.' "

In the same poem by Mr. Ewart we find a poet enquiring :

> " Blowing my trumpery trumpet,
> Looking for hounds for my horn,
> Shall I revert to ancient themes
> And wish I had never been born ? "

and an Ancient requesting us to

> " Deliver me from fornication and hockey."

We will, Mr. Ewart, we will !

Here we have certainly, if not lack of sense, a lack of any sense that is worth while—but to one reader, at least, it brings no compensation, definite or otherwise.

" Or is it," continues the City Editor, " Theodore Spencer ?

' Why can't we sleep a little more ? I'm sleepy,
Why can't we sleep a little more ? I'm sleepy,
Rattle shuffle ; rattle shuffle ;
Rattle shuffle ; rattle shuffle ;
The train's coming quickly
Coming
LOUDLY
Rattle shuffle rattle shuffle
STOP.' "

The members of Mr. and Mrs. Grigson's little
circle are not only poets and innovators, but wits.
Take, for instance, this poem, entitled, probably
with a view to disarming criticism, " Ballade
un peu Banale."

" The bellow of good Master Bull
    Astoundeth gentil Cow
    That standeth in the meadow cool
    Where cuckoo singeth now.

    She stoppeth in a moony trance
    Beneath the timeless trees,
    Where ebon-bellied shad-flies dance
    About her milk-white knees.

    He snuffeth her from distant field—
    Sly Farmer Pimp approves :
    To him the gates and latches yield :
    He smiles upon their loves.

    Bull boometh from the briary bush,
    Advances, tail aloft—
    The meadow grass is long and lush,
    The oozy turf is soft.

c

He stampeth with his foremost foot,
His nostrils breathing bale ;
Uncouth, unhallowed is his suit ;
The vestal turneth tail.

He feinteth with his ivory horn,
Bites rump, bites flank, bites nape—
Sweet Saviour of a Virgin born,
How shall this maid escape !

He chaseth her to pasture wall ;
She maketh stand, poor bird !
He wields his tail like an iron flail.
Alas ! he presseth hard !

I like to think sweet Jesus Christ,
For His dear Mother's sake,
By some miraculous device,
Her to Himself did take ;

That her preserv'd Virginity
Flutes holy flats and sharps
In that divine vicinity
Where Eliot's hippo harps."

How suitable is this tripping, slender, wilfully
winsome movement to the theme of the poem ! It
conveys so well the strength of the bull, does it not ?
Actually, we feel that we are watching the anæmic
loves of a pair of higher-thought folkdancers, glancing
roguishly at each other through their pince-nez.

Leaving aside the incompetence of the verse, shown
in this total unsuitability of treatment, and leaving
aside its coarseness, I should like to protest against
this trivial and vulgar little blasphemy being regarded as a work of art, and I protest against the impertinence of using Mr. Eliot's name in such a context.

In more serious moods we find Mr. and Mrs. Grigson enthroning deeply significant and evocative verse of this kind :

SLIDING TROMBONE.

" I have a little windmill on my head
Which draws up water to my mouth and eyes
When I am hungry or moved to tears
I have a little horn full of the odour of absinth
    in my ears
And on my nose a green parrakeet that flaps
    its wings
And cries ' aux armes '
When from the sky fall the seeds of the sun ;
The absence from the heart of steel
At the bottom of the boneless and stagnant
    realities
Is partial to crazy sea-fish
I am the captain and the alsatian at the cinema
I have in my belly a little agricultural machine
That reaps and binds electric flex
The cocoa-nuts thrown by the melancholy
    monkey
Fall like spittle into the water
Where they blossom again as petunias
I have in my stomach an ocarina and I have
    virginal faith
I feed my poet on the feet of a pianist
Whose teeth are even and uneven
And sad Sunday evenings
I throw my morganatic dreams
To the loving turtle-doves who laugh like hell."

G. RIBEMONT-DESSAIGNES
(Translated by David Gascoyne).

Even more advanced is the following " Poem in Seven Spaces."

POEM IN SEVEN SPACES.

2 golden
claws

a drop
of blood

the yellow
field of
folly

white   spiral
of wind upon
two great
        breasts

3 galloping black horses

the legs of
chairs break
with a dry
    crack

all objects have gone
far away and the sound
of a woman's steps and
the echo of her laugh
fade out of hearing

ALBERTO GIACOMETTI
(Translated by David Gascoyne).

No wonder that Mr. Grigson attaches importance to his own judgment as a critic. Of the " Poem in Seven Spaces," I can only say that I wish there had been more Spaces : in short, I wish there had been nothing excepting Space.

And now, after this brief but all sufficing Cook's Tour on the Continent under the guidance of Mr. and Mrs. Grigson, let us consider the criticisms in *New Verse.* Mr. Grigson and his " followers " (to quote an expression of the City Editor's) are nothing short of glorious as critics. Mr. Grigson, for instance, writing of Mr. Archibald MacLeish's " Conquistador," quotes these lines :

" That was the weight of their wild breath ;
    and they railed at him
Cursing the bed that bore the bum of his
    mother
And damning his father's fork for an ape's tail

And himself for the two-figged get of a goat
    and the brother of
Whores and a hare's scut and a bull's gear
And a gull and a kite : one first and another."

adding, gravely : " This is good " [for he is a man of the world, and nothing can surprise him] " but comparison, say, with Shakespearian imagery and word-use, for example :

' The Wren goes too't, and the small gilded Fly
Do's letcher in my sight. Let Copulation
    thrive.'

gives its shallowness away."

There is, of course, a slight difference.

Again, a " follower," Mr. Humphrey House, writing of Mr. Wyndham Lewis' " One Way Song " in *New Verse*, February, 1934, quotes these lines :

> " The man I am to blow the bloody gaff
> If I were given platforms ? The riff-raff
> May be handed all the trumpets that you will,
> Not so the golden-tongued, the window sill
> Is all the pulpit they can hope to get,
> Of a slum-garret, sung by Mistinguette,
> Too high up to be heard, too poor to attract
> Anyone to their so-called ' scurrilous ' tract."

and adds : " The above quotation not only illustrates Mr. Lewis' power as a rhetorician, but also affords a taste of his quality as an artist in words. *The affinity with Dryden is manifest.* The unforced, natural diction, the large virile utterance, are both there : so, too, I think, is the resonance, the ' gong-like note,' perhaps more obviously recognizable in such a line as

' No half-way house beyond the frosty bay.' "

Note.—The " affinity with Dryden " is such that in the last line the first alliterative B is placed, for no reason, in the wrong place, so that the line staggers and topples over !

" On other occasions," continues the " follower," " one is reminded of one of Dryden's latest direct descendants, Byron." A man who can compare Mr. Lewis' versification with that of Dryden, and a man who can call Byron a descendant of Dryden, will say anything !

"One Way Song " is, I believe, the only volume of poems by this distinguished writer in prose. It

is a little difficult to disentangle the central themes
of the poems in this book ; as difficult, indeed, as
to distinguish the events chronicled in the lines

" They told me you had been to her
And mentioned me to him,
You gave me a good character
But said I could not swim,—"

and the rest of that well-known poem.   One thing,
however, shines out very clearly from Mr. Lewis'
verse, and that is, that somebody has been behaving
pretty badly—*has not been kind !*

Now Mr. Lewis, in spite of all his boyish play-
fulness, in spite of that Boy Scout Movement for
Elderly Boys called " The Enemy," in spite of
being, as you might say, a Regular Pickle, has a
strong vein of sentimentality underlying all his
brusqueness.   Just as, in that long plaint " The
Apes of God," in the midst of worrying about the
wickedness of those who do, or do not, issue or
accept invitations to lunch, tea, or dinner, live in
studios, or pretend to be young, he could yet find
time to long for the unseen Mr. Pierpoint to be
not only feared, but *loved*—(this longing shows
itself in the conversation chez Kein)—so, in this
later work, Mr. Lewis longs for his friends to love
him, he longs to be *understood.*   Oh, will not
somebody be kind ?   This sentimentality, indeed,
masquerading as brusqueness, has grown to such a
pitch, both in " The Apes of God " and in this
book of poems, that we are reminded at moments
of a German jünges mädchen counting the petals
of a marguerite, pondering over the last words, the

last look, of the Herr Lieutenant, and longing, oh, more tenderly than anyone will ever, ever know, for him to turn from those wild, wild ways of his, and appreciate true worth! More often still we are reminded of a dear old lady howling denunciations of this person and of that, making a scene and " creating," as the servants say, because the Vicar no longer appreciates her church work, now that he has taken up with those *horrid* minxes who are a third of her age, and have thirty times her attractions. (" Lor, Mrs. Pipchin, love, how you *do* Create, to be sure! Now you sit down and have a good rest and a hot strong cup of tea, and then you'll feel better! ") But Mr. Lewis *will not* rest! He rejects the strong cup of tea and, egged on and sympathised with by such Powers and Portents as Mr. Montgomery Belgion and that Playboy of the West End, Mr. Augustus John, Mr. Lewis " creates," yelling defiance at those who do, or who do not, issue or accept invitation to lunch or dinner, underrate their ages, or live in studios. According to his own account, the " creations " in " The Apes of God " were received by a shower of mingled bouquets and brickbats. His life was, he assures us (Enemy Pamphlet, No. 1 : Satire and Fiction) threatened by an airman. But there were compensations. Mr. J. D. Beresford wrote from Ickleford Rectory admiring him. Dr. Meyrick Booth rolled down a flood of incense from Letchworth. Mr. Richard Aldington sent a verbal posy from Le Bouquet, Aiguebelle. Mr. Montgomery Belgion went so far as to say, " Here is the time philosophy routed entirely."

So much for this preceding work. But in the poems contained in "One Way Song" we find Mr. Lewis in a gentler mood. Oh, will not *somebody* be kind ? Who, he seems to enquire, in "If so the man you are," could be more amenable, was more formed to be loved ?

> "I'm not too careful with a drop of Scotch,
> I'm not particular about a blotch.
> I'm not alert to spy out a blackhead,
> I'm not the man that minds a dirty bed.
> I'm not the man to ban a friend because
> He breasts the brine in lousy bathing drawers.
> I'm not the guy to balk at a low smell,
> I'm not the man to insist on asphodel.
> This sounds like a He-fellow don't you think ?
> It sounds like that. I belch, I bawl, I drink."

In spite, however, of these soft allurements, in spite of all those endearing young charms, Mr. Lewis, according to himself, is not appreciated, though he even goes so far as to apologise for any little brusqueness that may have been noticed :

"I'm sorry if I've been too brutal, girls." Now, Mr. Lewis, not another word. Please. *I beg!* You know you ought not to spoil them. And besides, the pretty dears like your Cave-man stuff. For it is not often that they meet a real He-man. . . . And when they do. . . .

Yet consider for a moment, how Mr. Lewis is treated :

> "But lo upon the sidewalks of New York
> I am of the same standing as Montalk
> If that, of course. Spluttered in Cabala

It reaches me, the hiss of menacing blah.
Meanwhile, excluded, Snooty Baronet
Felt the full boycott, it is not sold yet,
Nor ever will be. . . ."

Too bad !

Leaving aside these natural grievances, much of
" One Way Song " is occupied with Time.

Now, Mr. Lewis resembles Cleopatra in this, if
in nothing else, that

" Age cannot wither him or custom stale
His infinite variety."

Yet, for some reason, he has a fear of Time. It
must be quite sixteen or seventeen years ago that
he said to me, in a very angry tone of voice :
" I am thirty-seven till I pass the word round.
D'you understand ? "

I said that I did, and I have obeyed his commands
implicitly ever since. To me, he will always be
thirty-seven.

In this book, however, we have Time as a
metaphysical concept, not as an enemy of another
kind ; and we find Mr. Lewis putting down his
foot very firmly about one matter :

" We must be frantically frontal "

he tells us, and we are warned about what will
happen if we are not.

Mr. Lewis suffers from various other little
troubles that he would like us to understand and
to sympathise with. There is, for instance, the
worry about backs and fronts to which I have
referred, and this, at moments, grows to such a

pitch that he seems scarcely to know if he is going
or coming.

" Try and walk backwards : you will quickly see
    How you were meant only *one-way* to be !
    Attempt to gaze out of your bricked-up back :
    You will soon discover what we *One-Ways* lack !
    Endeavour to reoccupy the Past :
    Your stubborn front will force you to stand fast !
    (No traffic caption of Sens Interdit
    Is necessary for this clearly One-Way Street.)
    Address yourself to sitting down front first—
    Your joints will stop you, or your hips will burst ! "

(Oh, will not *somebody understand ?*) Now, Mr.
Lewis, we *do* understand. And we want you to
know that you are amongst *friends*. You can
safely confide in us. We will stand by you. The
situation you describe must be most trying, but
these little things will occur, we know. And we
want you not to fret about the seriousness of the
symptoms.

We will now examine the comparison of " One
Way Song " with the poems of Dryden—and by
this we may gauge the worth of the criticism in
New Verse. Let us place these two poets in juxtaposition. Here is a passage from Mr. Lewis :

" I do not beg subscriptions for the sun—
    I come to levy imposts !   One by one
    I get into a row with angry persons
    Who cast upon my functions tart aspersions.
    Masks made of bast are useful, a ripsnorter
    Bursts in our faces, full of angry water
    And forked electricity.   What is the use

The indignant elements when they recuse
To menace with sunstroke ? I've had quite enough
Of heated argument about my stuff.
The long and the short of this is I am not
A doll of set responses in a fixed cot.
I go about and use my eyes, my tongue
Is not for sale—a little loosely slung
Perhaps but nothing more.   I esteem my role
To be grand enough to excuse me, on my soul,
From telling lies at all hours of the day !
Of saying the thing that is not, Swift would say,
If I am armed with bright invective, rare
That is, I agree—but mine is a *dangerous* affair."

This verse has, it is true, a certain rough energy—
a blustering vigour—and this is due to the fact that
Mr. Lewis has no use for anything that is not
essential. He is never redundant. But compare
those lines with the following passage from Dryden,
and we shall see that Mr. Lewis' texture is doughy
and inadequate. He can make no use of it.

" Of these the false Achitophel was first ;
A Name to all succeeding Ages curst :
For close Designs and crooked Counsels fit,
Sagacious, Bold, and Turbulent of wit,
Restless, unfixed in Principles and Place,
In Pow'r unpleased, impatient of Disgrace ;
A fiery Soul, which working out its way
Fretted the Pygmy Body to decay,
And o'er informed the Tenement of Clay ;
A daring Pilot in extremity ;
Pleas'd with the Danger, when the waves went high
He sought the Storms ; but, for a Calm unfit,

Would steer too nigh the Sands to boast his Wit.
Great wits are sure to Madness near alli'd,
And thin Partitions do their Bounds divide ;
Else, why should he, with Wealth and Honour blest,
Refuse his Age the needful hours of Rest ?
Punish a body which he could not please,
Bankrupt of Life, yet Prodigal of Ease ?
And all to leave what with his Toil he won
To that unfeather'd two-legged thing, a Son :
Got, while his Soul did huddled notions try,
And born a shapeless Lump, like Anarchy."

In this passage, where both the sound and the
imagery seem ruthless, ancient, and inevitable as
the clay after it was inundated by the Flood, the
force is gained, as it is sometimes gained in Pope's
satires, by the change from the softness of the
design of F's to the blows of succeeding hard
consonants. The triplet, in the most famous lines
of the whole passage :

> " A fiery soul, which working out its way
> Fretted the Pygmy Body to decay,
> And o'er informed the Tenement of Clay."

instead of weakening the heroic stanza, gives an
additional power and splendour, though this is
rarely the case where triplets are used. The
magnificence of the whole passage is added to by
the varying weights and the variations in rhythm
produced by the occasional alliteration. The movement of :

> " For close Designs and crooked Counsels fit"

seems, for instance, to be quite different from that of

" Punish a Body which he could not please,"

where the alliteration gives, at once, the impression
of an immense bulk straddling, and of a violent blow
given at the beginning and end of the line—a
blow which is repeated in the middle of the next
line :

" Bankrupt of Life, yet Prodigal of Ease."

The movement of this, again, seems to be quite
different from that of :

" In Pow'r unpleased, impatient of Disgrace."

And this differs from its preceding line :

" Restless, unfixed in Principles and Place,"

Yet all these lines (with the exception of the
famous triplet) are contained within the flawless
structure of the heroic couplet. Strength and
variation are gained by this absolute power over
alliteration. Great differences are effected, too, by
the varying height, depth, breadth and lightness
of the Cæsura.

In this line :

" In Pow'r unpleased, impatient of Disgrace,"

the effect is gained not only by the powerful
alliteration, but also by the phenomenal depth and
breadth of the Cæsura. Compare that line with
the succeeding couplet and half of a couplet :

" Of these the false Achitophel was first,
   A name to all succeeding Ages curst :
   For close Designs and crooked Counsels fit."

In this, the Cæsura hardly exists at all—at least it is so light as to be scarcely noticeable ; this lightness then changes into the violence (due to the depth of the pauses) in :

" Sagacious, Bold, and Turbulent of wit."

Though the violence of this is nothing to the violence of :

" In Pow'r unpleased, impatient of Disgrace."

.   .   .   .   .

" Bankrupt of Life, yet Prodigal of Ease "

—to return to that splendid line—possesses a Cæsura which, though long, yet (owing, I think, to the huddled three-syllabled word " Prodigal ") does not so much divide the line by a chasm, as produce a stretch of flat uninhabited land, and then melt into the rather terrible mock-jovial carelessness which is suitable to the subject.

As for the line :

" In Pow'r unpleased, impatient of Disgrace,"

the pause is of the same length as that in

" A fiery Soul, which working out its way,"

but in the last line quoted, owing to the softness of the F and S, the softness of the alliterative W's, the Cæsura, for some reason which I cannot explain (unless it be that " Soul " ends with a soft and lengthening L), seems more a matter of soaring through time, than a matter of chasm and violence. Texture appears, therefore, to have an effect upon the shape of the Cæsura.

When Dryden is describing stupidity, he frequently reduces the depth of the Cæsura—reduces it, practically, to non-existence, as in the line :

" Would steer too nigh the Sands to boast his Wit."

The reason for this is, I imagine, that he wishes to produce the impression that the subject of the line knows no division between light and darkness, between a spiritual mountain, gulf, or plain.

These satires are purposely thick, gross, terrible and blind as stupidity itself. Dryden's victims are not so much impaled (as are Pope's) in an everlasting moving heaving hell of lava, as made into a thick and world-wide mud-pudding (the supreme epitome of soulless matter) or buried alive beneath an immense rumbling fall of mountains. Dryden seems, not so much to rear himself to a world's height and crash down on his victims from the very heavens (like Pope), as to be in the state of Goya's " Giant Dancing." He treads on these insects, and they are gone. He has been at no effort to obliterate them.

Take this description of Og :

" Now stop your noses, Readers, all and some,
    For here's a tun work of Midnight to come,
    Og from a Treason Tavern rolling home
    Round as a globe, and Liquored every chink,
    Goodly and great he Sails behind his Link ;
    With all this Bulk there's nothing lost in Og,
    For ev'ry inch that is not Fool is Rogue ;
    A monstrous mass of foul corrupted matter
    As all the Devils had spew'd to make the batter."

That passage is inspired ; but the actual physical bludgeoning, whilst appalling in its effect, is done " on the level "—without physical effort. Here are gigantic muscles wiping out an insect—a rather fat one—without effort.

The unevenly arranged alliteration gives the impression of something thick and gross, rolling with drunkenness, and only kept on its feet by its very thickness, its meaningless bulk.

Occasionally, his antithesis is as violent as Pope's —as in :

" They got a Villain and we lost a Fool."

See, too, the effect he produces by internal and external rhymes in this quotation from " Absalom and Achitophel " :

" Not weighed or winnowed by the *multitude*,
But swallowed in the mass, *unchewed* and *crude*,
Some truth there was, but dashed and *brewed*
    with lies
To please the fools and puzzle all the wise."

The extraordinary force is gained, in part, by the balance brought about by the alliteration " weighed or winnowed " ; in part by the internal rhymes (the italics are mine) ; in part by the lifting sound of " dashed," and the still longer lifting sound, like that of a rising rage, of the " i " sound in " lies " and " wise."

These technical splendours, these giant muscles, capable of overturning a world, this extraordinary sensibility to texture, to the slightest variation—a sensibility so acute that I am reminded of the case

D

(reported to me by a friend who is a doctor) of a blind lady who, when walking in the country could tell if she was passing a hedge or a wall without touching them—these are unknown in the poetry of Mr. Lewis. His muscles are those of an ordinary man, though a man possessed of considerable talent for writing in prose. The muscular system of his verse, indeed, resembles that of Browning rather than of Dryden. There is nothing to be said about his technique. Yet he is compared to Dryden, who was one of the greatest technicians our race has known.

To such depths has the present state of criticism sunk.

CHAPTER II

GERARD MANLEY HOPKINS

WE have seen, in the first half of the preceding chapter, how the tactile sense, as well as energy and speed, were dying out of verse ; no longer was it regarded as necessary for a poet to be in command of his material, since that material was held to be of no importance. Poetry became, in some cases, like the Emperor's suit of clothes in the fairy tale, an imaginary covering to hide the nakedness of mankind and to shelter him from the cold—in other cases the suit of clothes was an actual suit, but it was of so threadbare a character, so outworn in cut and so faded in colour, that the fabric was worse than useless.

Yet in the midst of all this debility, lack of vitality, and threadbare texture, lived a great technical innovator, and a man whose senses were as acutely alive as those of any poet of our race. What an ironical fate was his ! Since it is very largely due to the influence of this poet's work (with that, also, of Donne) that the latest school of poets ascribe the trend of their verse, technic- ally. Yet no poet has been more alone, more " aristocratic," than both Hopkins and Donne ;

whereas the poets who imitate them dare not, or in any case do not, hunt the Infinite alone. They have gone back to primitive life, although they have lost the primitive senses : they hunt in packs, and the faces and the needs of their poems are the same.

In the threadbare minor poetry of the later Victorian and the Edwardian eras, though the technique of the art had recently been enriched by the innovations of Father Gerard Manley Hopkins, these had not yet had time to sink into the consciousness. But now, where these examples have been followed, they have not been understood, and Hopkins has met with the fate of nearly all innovators. It is a fact that Hopkins should never be regarded as a model, since he worked his own discoveries to the uttermost point ; there is no room for advancement, for development, along his lines. But leaving this truth aside it is a melancholy fact that his imitators have misunderstood his examples, and, ignorant that his rhythmical impetus, his magnificence of texture, are the results, at once natural and cultivated, of the properties of his material acted upon by the impact of his personality, they have produced poems with superimposed rhythms instead of rhythms inherent in the properties of the material. For not only have these poets lost their tactile sense, but (perhaps because of this loss) to them the resonance of all things are the same, they do not hear the difference in resonance between that of iron and of copper, as they do not feel the difference in texture between marble and stone, and, as for that, between the

different marbles.   Partly as a result of this insen-
sitiveness, they produce exterior, and therefore
unliving, rhythms, instead of rhythms which live
in, under, and over, the lines.   Imitations of
Hopkins have resulted, too, in a complete loss of
melody, arising from falsified, clumsy, or too-thick
vowel-schemes, clumsy and huddled-up assonance
patterns, useless alliterations, and a meaningless
accumulation of knotted consonants.*

Yet great (though incapable of further development) are the technical wonders from which these
imitations have sprung—these slandered originals
are full of significance.   Not, perhaps, since Dryden
and Pope have we had such mountains and gulfs,
such raging waves, such deserts of the eternal cold,
and these are produced not by a succession of
images alone, but by the movement of the lines,
by the texture, and by Hopkins' supreme gift of
rhetoric.   It should be realized that rhetoric is not
an incrustation, a foreign body which has somehow
transformed the exterior surface of a poem, dis-
tracting the mind from the main line ; it is, instead,
an immense fire breaking from the poem as from a
volcano.   Sometimes it is smooth, sometimes it is
fierce ; but the manner in which it is born is the
same.   " Decoration " in poetry does not exist ;
either the physical beauty has arisen from the
properties of the material, or the poem is a bad poem.

Hopkins was not understood by his contemporaries.   His friend Richard Watson Discon
perhaps alone assimilated and understood the
essence of this poetry, for in a letter to the poet

* See end of chapter.

he speaks of their temper, of their terrible quality, " something I cannot describe, but know to myself by the inadequate word ' terrible pathos,' something of what you call temper in poetry : a right temper which goes to the point of the terrible : the terrible crystal. Milton is the only one else who has anything like it, and he has it in a totally different way ; he has it through indignation, through injured majesty, which is a different thing."

Hopkins explains his rhythmical devices in the preface to his poems. He writes, for the most part, in a mixture of what he called Running Rhythm and Sprung Rhythm. Running Rhythm is the common English rhythm, and it is unnecessary to explain it in these pages : all that needs to be said is, that to gain variation, poets, when using it, have introduced licences of one kind and another, the principal being reversed feet and reversed rhythm. Should these variations be carried far enough—in short, to quote Hopkins himself : ". . . if you counterpoint throughout, since one only of the counter rhythms is actually heard, the other is really destroyed or cannot come to exist, and what is written is one rhythm only and probably sprung rhythm." As used by Hopkins, this measure has feet of from one to four syllables, and for particular effects any number of weak or slack syllables can be used. Each foot has one stress, and this falls on the only syllable should there be more than one. The feet are regular, measured in time, and any inequality they may seem to have is made up by pause and stressing.

In general, Sprung Rhythm is the most natural

of things. As Hopkins says : " (1) It is the rhythm
of common speech and of written prose, when
rhythm is perceived in them. (2) It is the rhythm
of all but the most monotonously regular music, so
that in the words of choruses and refrains and in
songs written closely to music it arises. (3) It is
found in nursery rhymes, weather saws, and so on ;
because, however these may have been once made
in running rhythm, the terminations having dropped
off by the change of language, the stresses come
together and so the rhythm is sprung. (4) It
arises in common verse when reversed or counter-
pointed, for the same reason."

We may see, therefore, that Sprung Rhythm is
not an innovation. Indeed, it is the rhythm of
Piers Ploughman and the rhythm of Skelton.
Greene, however, was the last poet who made use
of it, and Hopkins declares that since the Elizabethan
age, there is not a single, even short poem, in which
Sprung Rhythm is employed as a principle of
scansion.

Hopkins' rhythmical principles, which are based
on scholarship, arose, actually, from his feeling, his
instinct, and are thus in many ways the same as
those of such modern poets as Ezra Pound, Wilfred
Owen, and T. S. Eliot, men whose free verse arises
from feeling and intuition, but is guided by learning ;
this fact has been stated admirably by Professor
Herbert Read recently, in " Form in Poetry,"
and he points out, also, that " a second characteristic
of Hopkin's poetry which, while not so original,
is yet a cause of strangeness, may be found in his
vocabulary. No true poet hesitates to invent words

when his sensibility finds no satisfaction in current phrases. Words like " shinelight " and " firedint " are probably such inventions. But most of Hopkins's innovations are in the nature of new combinations of existing words, sometimes contracted similes or metaphors, and in this respect his vocabulary has a surface similarity to that of James Joyce. Examples of such phrases are to be found in almost every poem : " the beadbonny ash," " fallowboot fellow," " windlaced," " churls grace," " foot fretted," " clammyish lash tender combs," " wildsworth," etc.

Many of Hopkins' poems appear at first sight strange ; and this is due in part to his acute and strange visual sense, a sense which pierces down to the essence of the thing seen, and which, heightening the truth of it, by endowing it with attributes which at first seem alien, with colours that are sharper, clearer, more piercing than those that are seen by the common eye, succeeds in producing its inherent spirit. He does not obscure the thing seen by loading it with useless details, he produces the essence by giving one sharp visual impression, performing miracles by using comparisons which seem very remote, as when, for instance, in the lovely fragment that I am about to quote, he compares the fair hair of a youth to a sheaf of bluebells. This, to me, gives the fairness of the hair, and shows the straightness of it, and the way in which it flaps, for, of all flowers, only a sheaf of bluebells has this particular limpness. The fragment is one of an unfinished poem, and how innocent and gay and rustic is the movement of it.

" The furl of fresh-leaved dogrose down
His cheeks the forth-and-flaunting sun
Had swarthed about with lion-brown
Before the Spring was done.

His locks like all a ravel-rope's end,
With hempen strands in spray—
Fallow, foam-fallow, hanks—fall'n off their
    ranks,
Swung down at a disarray.

Or like a juicy and jostling shock
Of bluebells sheaved in May
Or wind-long fleeces on the flock
A day off shearing day.

Then over his turnèd temples—here—
Was a rose, or, failing that,
Rough-Robin or five-lipped campion clear
For a beauty-bow to his hat,
And the sunlight sidled, like dewdrops, like
    dandled diamonds,
Through the sieve of the straw of the plait."

Here we have a youth, in the midst of his walk,
suddenly leaping into the air and dancing for a
step or two, because of the fun of being alive on
this lovely and unfading summer morning. The
innocent and sweet movement of this very lovely
fragment is due, partly, to the skilful interposition
of an extra syllable from time to time, and an
occasional rare internal rhyme ; and the clearness
and poignant colours of the morning are conveyed
by the sounds of " juicy," " bluebells," " sheaved,"

with their varying degrees of deep and piercing colour.

This acute and piercing visual apprehension, this sharpening and heightening of the thing seen, so as to obtain its essential spirit, is found again in these lines from " The May Magnificent " :

> " Ask of her, the mighty mother :
> Her reply puts this other
> Question : what is Spring ?
> Growth in everything—
>
> Flesh and fleece, fur and feather,
> Grass and greenworld all together,
> Star-eyed strawberry-breasted
> Throstle above her nested
>
> Cluster of bugle blue eggs thin
> Forms and warms the life within ;
> And bird and blossom swell
> In sod or sheath or shell.
>
> .   .   .   .   .
>
> When drop-of-blood and foam-dapple
> Bloom lights the orchard apple
> And thicket and thorp are merry
> With silver-surfèd cherry.
>
> And azuring-over greybell makes
> Wood banks and brakes wash wet like lakes
> And magic cuckoocall
> Caps, clears, and clinches all.
>
> This ecstasy all through mothering earth
> Tells Mary her mirth till Christ's birth
> To remember and exultation
> In God who was her salvation."

In the sharply-seen image of the " star-eyed strawberry-breasted " thrush—strawberry-breasted because of the freckles on her breast—in the enhanced and deepened colour of the " bugle blue eggs," in which the sharp U of " bugle " melting to the softer U of " blue " gives the reflection and the sisterhood of the deep blue heaven, the flower, and the egg, shifting and changing in the clear light, in the acutely-seen " greybells," we have the same piercing, truth-finding vision that produced for us the fair hair of the country youth.

But now we must turn from this exquisite and youthful happiness, this unfading spring weather, to the " terrible " poems.   Let us take, to begin with, the first verse of that great poem, " The Wreck of the Deutschland " :

> " Thou mastering me
> God ! giver of breath and bread ;
> World's strand, sway of the sea ;
> Lord of living and dead ;
> Thou hast bound bones and veins in me,
>   fastened me flesh,
> And after it almost unmade, what with dread,
> Thy doing : and dost thou touch me afresh ?
> Over again I feel thy finger and find thee."

In this passage we have the huge primeval swell of the sea, with its mountain-heights and its hell-depths, we have the movement before life began, conveyed by technical means.

In the slow and majestic first line, the long and strongly-swelling vowels, and the alliterative M's, produce the sensation of an immense wave gathering

itself up, rising slowly, ever increasing in its huge
power, till we come to the pause that follows the
long vowel of " me." Then the wave falls, only to
rush forward again.

After this majestic line comes the heaving line

"God! giver of breath and bread,"

ending with the ship poised on the top of the wave.
This last effect is caused by the assonances of
" breath and bread." The sound of " breath " is
slightly longer, has slightly more of a swell beneath
the surface than "bread," because of the "th." This
pause on the top of the wave is followed by the
gigantic straining forward of the waves in the line

" World's strand, sway of the sea,"

an effect that has been produced by the strong
alliterative S's, reinforced by the internal R's of
" World's strand," followed by the internal W of
" sway." This line, after the huge tossing up and
down from the dulled A of " strand " to the higher
dissonantal A of " sway," ends by sweeping forward
still further with the long vowel-sound of " sea," a
sound that is more peaceful than that of " strand "
and " sway " because of the absence of consonants.

The whole poem is inhabited by a gigantic and
overwhelming power, like that of the element that
inspired it. The huge force produced by the
alliteration in the lines I have analysed above, and
in such a line as

" Thou hast bound bones and veins in me,
        fastened me flesh,"

has rarely been exceeded, even by Dryden and by
Pope, those masters of the effects that can be
produced by alliteration. It is true that the last
line I have quoted from Hopkins is necessarily,
because of its subject, more static than most of the
more magnificent lines of Dryden and of Pope, yet
Hopkins' line is of nearly an equally giant stature.
At the end of this verse, the huge primeval power,
splendour and terror which inhabit it change to the
softness and tenderness of

" Over again I feel thy finger and find thee,"

a line which is equalled in gentleness and sweetness
by the lovely line in the ninth verse :

" Thou art lightning and love, I found it, a
winter and warm."

How huge is the contrast between this and the
black coldness and opaqueness, like that of savage
waters, of the line

" And the sea flint-flake, black-backed in the
regular blow,"

The opaqueness of this is caused by the flat
assonances, the thick consonants, of " black-backed "
and " blow."

In the same verse, we find this line :

" Wiry and white-fiery and whirlwind-swivelled
snow."

I cannot recall any other English poet who has
produced such a feeling of huge and elemental cold
as Hopkins, a cold that is sometimes devouring,

sometimes dulled. In the line quoted above, Hopkins produces the sensation of watching a wave receding and then plunging forward, by rhyming the first and the fourth word. A higher and more piercing dissonantal I precedes the second rhyme, and this feeling of the wave plunging forward is the result, too, of the internal R's, which always either lengthen a word or else make it flutter. In this case (as in the line

" World's strand, sway of the sea "),

they lengthen it, or rather give the feeling of an immeasurable force driving forward.

This relentless and inevitable wave-stretch, this driving forward, contained in the sound of " whirl " is followed immediately by the shrinking sound of " wind," the I's in " wind " and " swivelled " being dull with cold.

We find an equally world-huge, overwhelming coldness in this quotation from " The Loss of the Euridice " :

" A beetling baldbright cloud through England
    Riding : there did storms not mingle ?   and
    Hailropes hustle and grind their
    Heavengravel ?   Wolfsnow, worlds of it, wind
        there ? "

In this, our very bones seem ground and beaten by the ropes of the harsh hail. The effect may, or may not, be partly due to the grinding harshness of the " grind " " heavengravel " sounds, and to the long-sustained high internal rhymes " grind " and " wind." The imagery is, however, mainly responsible for the magnificence of the verse—the huge imagination, the deep consciousness that inspired the phrase " Wolfsnow, worlds of it, wind there."

How tremendous is the difference between this overwhelming universe of the cold, and the ripeness, the fullness, the flooding of the whole being, conveyed by this passage about a heart filled with the contemplation of Christ's Passion.

After the passage :

" The dense and the driven Passion, and frightful
        sweat ;
Thence the discharge of it, there it's swelling
        to be,
Though felt before, though in high flood yet—
What none would have known of it, only the
        heart, being hard at bay,"

come these lines :

    " Is out with it !   Oh,
We lash with the best or worst
Word last !   How a lush-kept plush-capped sloe
Will, mouthed to flesh-burst
Gush !—flush the man, the being with it, sour
        or sweet,
Brim, in a flash, full !—Hither then, last or first,
To hero of Calvary, Christ's feet—
Never ask if meaning it, wanting it, warned of
        it—men go."

I do not care, personally, for these lines, because I find the substance too rich, too thick, for my taste. But the richness is deliberate : the thick gushing of the ripe blood is intentional.

A lovely movement, a sense that all is well, that all creation is part of a controlled and gigantic design, is given by the internal rhymes and assonances of :

" For, how to the heart's cheering
   The down-dugged ground-hugged grey
   Hovers off, the jay-blue heavens appearing
   Of pied and peeled May !
   Blue-beating and hoary glow-height ; or night,
      still higher,
   With belled fire and the moth-soft Milky Way,
   What by your measure is the heaven of desire,
   The treasure never eyesight got, nor was ever
      guessed what for the hearing?"

The movement of this is like that of a bird flying through the bright air, swooping downward to its nest, then up again through the holy and peaceful light.

We find a lovely floating movement, but this time not like that of a bird flying home through the wide air, but, instead, like that of a bird seeking its nest through the soft dark leaves of a wood, in " Peace "—a poem which must be quoted whole in order to do its beauty justice.

" When will you ever, Peace, wild wooddove,
      shy wings shut,
   Your roaming round me end, and under be
      my boughs ?
   When, when, Peace, will you, Peace ? I'll not
      play hypocrite
   To own my heart : I yield you do come some-
      times ; but

That piecemeal peace is poor peace. What pure
    peace allows
Alarms of war, the daunting wars, the death
    of it ?

O surely, reaving Peace, my Lord should leave
    in lieu
Some good ! and so he does leave Patience
    exquisite,
That plumes to Peace thereafter. And when
    Peace does house
He comes with work to do, he does not come
    to coo,
He comes to brood and sit."

It is owing to the reiterations, and to the subtle
arrangement of the exquisitely soft and hardly
perceptible variations of the O and U sounds
(" wood," " you," " do," " poor," " pure," " good,"
" plumes," " coo " and " brood ") with their higher
dissonances " round " and " boughs " that we see
the dove circling through the trees, seeking its
home—that we hear its soft warm voice. In this
beautiful poem the form, the texture and the
subject form one miraculous whole.

To take another poem, " Binsey Poplars," though
it is less lovely than " Peace," yet here again the
texture and movement are born from the needs of
the subject. This suitability is particularly exquisite
in the first verse :

" My aspens dear, whose airy cages quelled,
    Quelled or quenched in leaves the leaping sun,
    All felled, felled, are all felled ;

E

Of a fresh and following folded rank
    That spared, not one,
    That dandled a sandalled
Shadow that swam or sank
On meadow and river and wind-wandering weed-
    winding bank."

A lovely air blows through these lines, produced by the wandering and fluctuating length of the lines, and by the fact that " weed-winding " is a higher, and slightly slower, echo of " wind-wandering." The alliterative Qu sounds give us the feeling of dew-laden leaves. This effect of dew on leaves can be produced by many different sounds, but in each case the warmth or chilliness of the leaves, the freshness or darkness varies. As I said in my first volume of " The Pleasures of Poetry," Milton's line :

" While the still morn went out with sandals grey "

conveys the sense of dew dropping from the leaves, so different in surface and in smell, and of summer air breathing, by the use of scarcely separated L's, by the dissonance of " while " and " still."

If we compare the exquisite lightness and airiness and subtlety of " Binsey Poplars " with the terror and huge strength of " Carrion Comfort "—perhaps the greatest of Hopkins' sonnets—we shall see the variety of which he is capable.

" Not, I'll not, carrion comfort, Despair, not
    feast on thee ;
Not untwist—slack they may be—these last
    strands of man

In me, or, most weary, cry *I can no more.* I can ;
Can something, hope, wish day come, not choose
    not to be.
But ah, but O thou terrible, why wouldst thou
    rude on me
Thy wring-world right foot rock ? lay a lionlimb
    against me ? scan
With darksome devouring eyes my bruisèd bones ?
    and fan,
O in turns of tempest, me heaped there ; me
    frantic to avoid thee and flee ?

Why ? that my chaff might fly ; my grain lie,
    sheer and clear.
Nay in all that toil, that coil, since (seems) I
    kissed the rod,
Hand rather, my heart lo ! lapped strength, stole
    joy ; would laugh, cheer.
Cheer whom though ? the hero whose heaven-
    handling flung me, foòt tròd
Me ? or me that fought him ? O which one ? is
    it each one ? that night, that year
Of now done darkness I wretch lay wrestling with
    (my God !) my God."

The great strangeness of this poem is almost
entirely a matter of texture. He recognized this
strangeness in nearly all his poems, for we find him
writing to a friend in a letter dated 1879 : " No
doubt my poetry errs on the side of oddness.
I hope in time to have a more balanced and
Miltonic style. But as air, melody, is what strikes
me most of all in music, and design in painting,
so design, pattern or what I call inscape is what I,

above all, aim at in poetry. Now it is the virtue
of design, pattern, or inscape to be distinctive,
and it is the vice of distinctiveness to become queer.
This vice I cannot have escaped." Later we find
him explaining. . . . " Moreover, the oddness may
make them repulsive at first sight, and yet Lang
might have liked them on second reading. Indeed,
when, on somebody returning me the Euridice, I
opened and read some lines, as one commonly reads
whether prose or verse, with the eyes, so to say
only, it struck me aghast with a kind of raw nakedness and unmitigated violence I was unprepared
for : but take breath and read it with the ears, as
I always wish to read, and my verse becomes
all right."

It is exactly in this raw nakedness and unmitigated
violence, in a sort of leonine majesty, that Hopkins'
greatness was shown.

But now we come to his tragedy—one which
befalls nearly every great poet—the weak imitators
of his strangeness, his technical splendours. Mr.
Charles Williams, in his introduction to the new
edition of Hopkins' poems, says that Gerard Hopkins
was " not the child of vocabulary but of passion."
His imitators are the children of vocabulary alone.
In one of his lectures on Shakespeare, Coleridge
defined the need for *inherent* form thus :

" No work of true genius dares want its appropriate form, neither indeed is there any danger of
this. As it must not, so genius cannot, be lawless :
for it is even this that constitutes its genius—the
power of acting creatively under laws of its own
origination." In this definition we find the

condemnation of these imitators of Hopkins, whose
rhythms, whose vocabulary, are unnatural to the
subject. Here we have one example by Mr.
Charles Madge—lines which evidently arose from
a misunderstanding of Hopkins' methods :

" Master to me : fly turning clouds to walls
Approaching steep to life if that is square.

The hold on me of the held-onto hand
Shows where bone lies, and if I ever knew
The touched quick once, big now is here instead.

Given this morning not more true or untrue
Than the known inspiration of air
Something which is muscular to have said
A rock or wingbrace to understand
Between standing-room and space that falls.

The step on step of incident is where
Is the heard voice of blood that calls and calls."

                                            etc.

Here we have all Hopkins' difficulty, and obscurity, but none of his strength, of his vitality, of
his acute visual sense. The fragment lies dead on
the page, and the rest of the poem is in no way
more vital. Here, too, is another misassimilation
of Hopkins by the same writer, and this poem has
been " enthroned " by Mr. or Mrs. Grigson : The
poem is called " On Going Down " and I shall
only quote enough to show the quality of the whole :

" Oh hated silence, when the end of time
Bears on us down, and we go down, unclimb

What have been an assent, should shoulder high
Towards what would.   But being sent down, I
Remain no word to say
And so slow still heard shouting streams away."

The rest of the poem is just the same, and I, too, " remain no word to say," excepting to enquire, wearily : Sent down *where ?* Sent down whence ? To the bargain basement in a lift, or from Oxford or Cambridge ?

But the worst example I have found is one from a poem the author of which, to my great regret, is a young critic for whom I have much admiration, so I shall not, for this reason, give his name. Dr. Leavis has singled out this lumpy, ugly, clumsy verse for high praise, and ascribes it to the influence of Mr. Eliot and of Donne, but I find in it more of the (misunderstood) influence of Hopkins.

" Law *makes long spokes* of the *short stakes* of men
Your well-fenced out real estate of mind
No high flat of the nomad citizen
Looks over, or train leaves behind.

Your rights extend under and above your claim
Without bound ; you own land in Heaven and
Hell ;
Your part is of *earth's surface* and *mass* the same
Of all *cosmos' volume*, and all stars as well."

(The italics are mine.) These verses almost defeat criticism. I will leave out of the question the hideous internal rhyme and dissonance scheme of the first line, and the still more hideous assonances and dissonances of " without bound ; you own

land " and " cosmos' volume," with the mud-dark
sound of the last two quoted words. I will leave
out of the question the thick, sticky, treacly
agglomeration of S's in the first and seventh lines,
and will content myself with remarking that there
is a slight unnecessary unnatural space (not a
cæsura) inhabited by a minute sticky, dragging-
upward movement, after " makes " and " spokes "
and between " short " and " stakes," a pause and
movement that remind me of a fly lifting its feet
out of a treacle jar. In the line " Your well-fenced
out real estate of mind," half a syllable is missing,
so that there is a gap between " out " and " real."
This missing half-syllable is *added* to the line,
" Your rights extend under and above your claim "
(here is no question of pretended elision. The
" d " in " under " prevents that), so that in this
line the fly seems to make a very unsuccessful but
plucky attempt to spread his wings and flutter, and
finally, in the phrase " cosmos' volume," this victim .
of sweetness gives a final heave, and, one mass of
thick treacle, falls at our feet.

Dr. Leavis admiringly ascribes these technical
horrors to the influence of Mr. Eliot and Donne,
saying : " To those sympathetic to the present
view of this book [' New Bearings '] Donne is one
of the greatest masters of technique who ever
lived. . . . But it will not do to let this reference
to Donne imply a misleading account of Mr. ——
[the writer of the fragment quoted above]. He
is very original ; not only his ideas but his attitude
towards them and his treatment of them are
modern." They are, indeed, and I think one can

trace more of the influence of Hopkins, technically, than that of Donne or of Mr. Eliot.

Dr. Leavis adds : " His verse always has a rich and strongly characteristic life, for he is intensely interested in his technique as in his ideas "—and from the Doctor's pages arises a loud buzzing about " intelligence and technical skill," with one note of faint regret that " in his work the heat of creation is as yet too exclusively a matter of interest in technique and ideas." We are warned that " in the present phase of English poetry, Mr. —— [the author in question] should be paid the closest attention."

What nonsense is this !

How long, O Lord. . . .

CHAPTER III

WILLIAM BUTLER YEATS

As we have seen in the first chapter of this book, the poetry which followed that of Swinburne, the two Rossettis and Tennyson, was flat and thin, or shallow and shadowless. The weak imitators of these poets had determined to *create* a poetry—their poetry never grew, it was formed by their nerveless and numb fingers—which, if it could not provide an escape from life, since it had not the potency of a drug, could provide a polite excuse for not facing life at the moment, an evasion like the phrase " Not at Home."

In order to add strength to this illusion of having evaded life, flat match board partitions formed of splinters from works of the great poets, carefully glued together, were set up. Many examples of this fashion are to be found at the end of the " Oxford Book of English Verse," and the following sonnet, by Andrew Lang—" The Odyssey "—is a typical specimen :

" As one that for a weary space has lain
  Lull'd by the song of Circe and her wine
  In gardens near the pale of Proserpine,
  Where the Ææan isle forgets the main,
  And only the low lutes of love complain,

And only shadows of wan lovers pine—
As such an one were glad to know the brine
Salt on his lips, and the large air again—
So gladly from the songs of modern speech
Men turn, and see the stars, and feel the free
Still wind beyond the close of heavy flowers,
And through the music of the languid hours
They hear the Ocean on a western beach
The surge and thunder of the Odyssey."

It must be admitted that whatever sound *is* heard through the music of this particular languid hour—which seems more like a century of weariness, in spite of the allottèd space of a sonnet—we certainly do not hear the surge and thunder of the Odyssey. What we hear, actually, are thin echoes of the voices of certain more recent poets, weakened by death.

In the third line we have a debilitated echo of Swinburne, in the fourth an invalid echo of Shelley, in the fifth line and at the end of the eleventh, we have a hotch-potch of the kind of verse that Swinburne and Rossetti would have written if they had had no gift for poetry, and if they had had medicinal water in their veins instead of fiery blood. The sixth line pays an unfortunate and irritating compliment to Keats, and the whole poem is sprinkled with a little watered-down Tennyson.

Polite evasions and complimentary excuses of this kind moved side by side with a false simplicity and a complete breakdown of rhythm, and this was not a purposeful breakdown, due to a wish to show the laming of spiritual purpose in the modern world, but was the result of a lack of adhesion in the separate parts which, again, was due to a lack of purpose in the poet, or was the result of a nerveless incapacity to grasp or to handle the material of poetry.

Then, in the midst of this false simplicity and false grandeur, in the midst of this blankness and nullity, arose a great poet, one who was to " give a tongue to the sea-cliffs."

Note. – See " Autobiographies," W. B. Yeats.

In this great poet's veins poetry grew like a rose, unfolding its dark secrets within his blood, colouring his veins with the beauty and richness of its nature.

With Mr. Yeats, poetry meant no escape from life ; poetry *was* life—it was action as much as dream—and dream was a part of life, a refreshment, and a re-flowering. He believed in the unity of all lives :

" I had been put into a rage by the followers of Huxley, Tyndall, Carolus Duran, and Bastien Lepage, who not only asserted the unimportance of subject whether in art or literature, but the independence of the arts from one another. Upon the other hand, I delighted in every age where poet and artist confined themselves gladly to some inherited subject—matter known to the whole people, for I thought that in man and race alike there is something called ' Unity of Being ' using that term as Dante used it when he compared beauty in the Convito to a perfectly proportioned human body. My father, from whom I learned the term, preferred a comparison to a musical instrument so strung that if we touch a string all the strings murmur faintly."

Note. – "Autobiographies," page 235.

This unity of Being, this proportion of loveliness, is to be found in all Mr. Yeats' poems, grown, as they are, out of the depths of belief, flowering from the blood in his veins.

His genius is Belief that has found its natural form in a perfect proportion of beauty, unstained by Time, since Time has brought only its peaceful-ness, not its darkness, to this beauty. Here, indeed, we have one on whom the shadows of much earthly loveliness have fallen, and who has known the radiance of eternity and the wisdom that lies hidden in the heart of darkness.

At the beginning of his life, he knew the experiences of which Gerard de Nerval wrote ; but Mr. Yeats' awareness was deeper, the transcendental forms into which his experiences were transmitted cannot be likened to the beautiful illusions of reality which grew from poor de Nerval's darkened mind, and which formed his loveliest poems. Yet the passage from de Nerval which Mr. Arthur Symons quotes in his " Symbolism in Literature " might refer to Mr. Yeats in his earlier days :

" Things without form and without life lent themselves to the designs of my mind ; out of combinations of stones, the fissures of angles, crevices or openings, the shape of leaves, out of colours, odours, and sounds, I saw unknown harmonies come forth. ' How is it,' I said to myself, ' that I can possibly have lived so long outside nature, without identifying myself with her.' All things live, all things are in motion, all things correspond ; the magnetic rays emanating from myself or others

traverse without obstacle the infinite chain of created
things ; a transparent network covers the world,
whose loose threads communicate more and more
closely with the planets and the stars. Now a
captive upon the earth, I held converse with the
starry choir."

Mr. Symons wrote of de Nerval that he had thus
" realized the central secret of the mystics, from
Pythagoras   onwards,   the   secret   which   the
Smaragdine Tablet of Hermes betrays in its ' as
things are below, so are they above ' which Boehme
has classed in his teaching of signatures and
Swedenborg has systematized in his doctrine of
correspondences."

If this is true of Gerard de Nerval, it is true also
of Mr. Yeats, who has found this " central truth "
after plunging, as he tells us in his " Autobiographies," " into a labyrinth of images, into that
labyrinth that we are warned against in those
Oracles which antiquity has attributed to Zoroaster,
but modern scholarship to some Alexandrian poet.
' Stoop not down to the darkly splendid world wherein
lieth continually a faithless depth and Hades wrapped
in cloud, delighting in unintelligible images.' "

In his heart, in his mind, in his spirit, before his
eyes, was an ideal, a purpose from which he could
not be shaken, which had accompanied him into the
labyrinth and through the darkly splendid world
wherein lieth continually a faithless depth. . . .

In a time when Villiers de l'Isle Adam could
write " as for living, our servants will do that for us,"
Mr. Yeats was planning " A Mystical Order " (see

"Autobiographies," page 314) " which should buy or
hire the castle, and keep it as a place where its
members could retire for a while from the world,
and where we might establish mysteries like those
of Eleusis and Samothrace ; and for ten years to
come my most impassioned thought was a vain
attempt to find philosophy and create ritual for
that Order. I had an unshakeable conviction,
arising how or whence I cannot tell, that invisible
gates would open as they opened for Blake, as they
opened for Boehme, and that this philosophy
would find its manuals of devotion in an imaginative
literature, and set before Irishmen for special manual
an Irish literature which, though made by many
minds, would seem the work of a single mind, and
turn our places of beauty or legendary association
into holy symbols. I did not think this philosophy
would be altogether pagan, for it was plain that its
symbols must be selected from all those things that
had moved men most during many, mainly Christian
centuries."

With this belief in his heart, one who was to " give
a tongue to the sea-cliffs " created the poems, each
of which, to paraphrase a saying of Mallarmé, " is
an entire word remade out of many vocables, new,
unknown to the language."

It is forty-five years since the earliest of these
great poems gave new life to the language, and
today they spring into our consciousness anew, as
if we heard them for the first time ; and the wonders
and splendours of the latest poems are even greater,
since they have grown from a deeper wisdom, a
more universal experiment.

Mr. Yeats has said, of certain of the earliest poems with a rhythm that still echoed Morris " I prayed to the Red Rose, to Intellectual Beauty," but that echo sounds in his mind alone. To all other ears, his poems have had always the strangeness, the identity, of great poetry, as we shall see from the following poem, " He hears the Cry of the Sedge," from the earliest book of all, " The Wind in the Reeds."

> " I wander by the edge
>   Of this desolate lake
>   Where wind cries in the sedge :
>   *Until the axle break*
>   *That keeps the stars in their round,*
>   *And hands hurl in the deep*
>   *The banners of East and West,*
>   *And the girdle of light is unbound,*
>   *Your breast will not lie by the breast*
>   *Of your beloved in sleep.*"

A strange coldness and desolation is produced, in this lovely poem, by the sudden shifting of the accents and by the fluctuations in the strength or breath of these—is caused, too, by the fact that the second line seems shrunken as to length, but yet has a sudden sweep outwards owing to the long cold A of " lake." The eighth and ninth lines are suddenly blown outwards, as if by a wind, but the tenth dies away again slowly into a long stretch of silence.

The strange cold faery-like air which haunts this poem is produced, also, by the changes of speed between the one-syllabled, two-syllabled and three-syllabled words, and by the fact that in some of the two-syllabled words the second syllable dies or sinks or withers into silence, whereas in " unbound " each syllable is a long stretch of sound, and in " wonder " the first syllable is dark, dim and long, and the second dies away but slowly.

From time to time, also, a strange echo sighs within the lines, as here :

> " *I* wander *by* the edge
> Of this desolate lake
> Where wind *cries* in the sedge : "

and here :

> " That *keeps* the stars in their round,
> And *hands* hurl in the *deep*
> The *banners* of East and West,
> And the girdle of *light* is unbound,
> Your breast will not *lie* by the breast
> Of your beloved in sleep."

Let us take now the strange and unexplainable magic of " The Old Men Admiring Themselves in the Water "—a poem which is dated a few years later than the previous poem—in 1904 :

> " I heard the old, old men say,
> ' Everything alters,
> And one by one we drop away ! '
> They had hands like claws, and their knees
> Were twisted like the old thorn trees
> By the waters.

I heard the old, old men say,
' All that's beautiful drifts away
Like the waters.' "

The strange beauty of this miraculous little
poem is not to be explained ; it is not due alone
to the association between the idea of

" their knees
Were twisted like the old thorn trees,"

and the idea of the fading water-frail trembling
beauty of the flowers on those trees—trembling
like the sound of " everything alters," dying away
like the sound of " By the waters." Nor is the
beauty due only to the strange assonance of " alters "
with " waters "—and to the fact that " alters " is
really, owing to the L, a less clear echo of " waters,"
although it precedes the sound of " waters "—so
that it seems, almost, a memory which brings back
the reality, or a reflection shaken in the water.
Nor is the strangeness due only to the echo

" By the waters "

" Like the waters. . . ."

Both these lovely and flawless poems are inhabited,
as I have said, by a strange cold faery-like air.
This peculiar beauty had not found its way into
poetry before the advent of Mr. Yeats, excepting
in " La Belle Dame sans Merci " ; but Mr. Yeats'
earlier poems are pale with dew, and sigh like birds
from an unknown country, telling us legends in an
unknown tongue. Yet their inherent life, for all

F

this strangeness, is so complete that our life seems dim in their presence.

Few artists can have given us so complete a record of the life of their soul—a record which is clothed in reticence and moves with a supreme dignity—as that given us by Mr. Yeats in his "Autobiographies" and in the "Essays." Take, for instance, this passage in which all the patience of a great artist is conveyed: "I was about to learn that if a man is to write lyric poetry he must be shaped by nature and art to some one out of half a dozen traditional poses, and be lover or saint, sage or sensualist, or mere mocker of all life; and that none but that stroke of luckless luck can open before him the accumulated expression of the world. And this thought before it could be knowledge was an instinct." ("Autobiographies," page 105.)

The search for wisdom, the thirst for God—the dedication of his poetry, pure and impassioned, and flawless in its melodic line, to the ideal that ruled his life—we may find this record of the search for the Grail in "Autobiographies."

"I was unlike others of my generation in one thing only. I am very religious, and deprived by Huxley and Tyndall, whom I detested, of the simple-minded religion of my childhood, I had made a new religion, almost an infallible church of poetic tradition, of a fardel of stories, and of personages and emotions, inseparable from their first expression, passed on from generation to generation by poets and painters with some help from philosophers and theologians. I wished for a world, where I could discover this tradition perpetually, and not in pictures and in poems only, but in tiles round the chimney piece and in the hangings that kept out the draught. I had even created a dogma : ' Because those imaginary people are created out of the deepest instinct of man, to be his measure and his norm, whatever I can imagine those mouths speaking may be the nearest I can go to truth.' "

He had come to hate Victorian science, he tells us (" Autobiographies," page 101), " with a monkish hate," for he thirsted for that wisdom which is a voice of God.

His poetry is a universal poetry, that speaks to all men, although his voice is that of the sea-cliffs of Ireland, of the sedge of the lakes of Ireland . . . " from the moment I began the ' Wanderings of Usheen '," he tells us in a note, " . . . my subject matter became Irish." His voice is an Irish voice, but it speaks of a universal wisdom that existed in the beginning of things ; and that wisdom was sought in many ways and on many paths :

" I filled my mind with the popular beliefs of Ireland. . . . I sought some symbolic language reaching far into the past and associated with familiar names and conspicuous hills that I might not be alone amid the obscure impressions of the senses . . . or mourned the richness or reality lost to Shelley's ' Prometheus Unbound ' because he had not discovered in England or in Ireland his Caucasus. . . ." (" Essays," page 434.)

How deep is the wisdom of this poem, and how intense and strange its identity :

The Three Hermits.

" Three old hermits took the air
By a cold and desolate sea,
First was muttering a prayer,
Second rummaged for a flea ;
On a windy stone, the third,
Giddy with his hundredth year,
Sang unnoticed like a bird :
' Though the Door of Death is near
And what waits behind the door,
Three times in a single day
I, though upright on the shore,
Fall asleep when I should pray.'
So the first, but now the second :
' We're but given what we have earned
When all thoughts and deeds are reckoned,
So it's plain to be discerned
That the shades of holy men
Who have failed, being weak of will,
Pass the Door of Birth again,
And are plagued by crowds, until
They've the passion to escape.'
Moaned the other, ' They are thrown
Into some most fearful shape.'
But the second mocked his moan :
' They are not changed to anything,
Having loved God once, but only
To a poet or a king
Or a witty lovely lady.'
While he'd rummaged rags and hair,

> Caught and cracked his flea, the third,
> Giddy with his hundredth year,
> Sang unnoticed like a bird."

The strange beauty of this poem does not lie alone in the knowledge that it is sung on the shore of eternity—

> (" By a cold and desolate sea ") . . .

The beggar (who " rummaged rags and hair
> Caught and cracked his flea) "

has turned over, sorted and summed up all the remnants of mortality and has found life—in one form. The praying beggar fears the approaching sleep ; but beside them is the strange saint-like ecstasy of one who

> " Giddy with his hundredth year,
> Sang unnoticed like a bird "—

and who, like a bird, trusts in the love of God.

Here already, the old men are faced with a more bitter, a bleaker wind than that which sounds among the thorn-trees. And in all these strangely beautiful, proud poems, in which all life is compressed into the image of a beggar or of a tree, in which a black stone can hold all the secrets of the heart, a cold wind blows from the shores of eternity. The beings of whom Mr. Yeats writes, though they bear names we know, and though we might call to them with our mortal voices, exist in eternity and not in time ; their age is not the age of dust alone :

> " Laughter not time destroyed my voice
> And put that crack in it,

And when the moon's pot-bellied
I get a laughing fit,
For that old Madge comes down the lane
A stone upon her breast,
And a cloak wrapped about the stone,
And she can get no rest
With singing hush and hush-a-bye ;
She that has been wild
And barren as a breaking wave
Thinks that the stone's a child.

And Peter that had great affairs
And was a pushing man,
Shrieks ' I am King of the Peacocks,'
And perches on a stone ;
And then I laugh till tears run down
And the heart thumps at my side,
Remembering that her shriek was love
And that he shrieks from pride."

Note.—" A Man Young and Old " : VII—" The Friends of his Youth."

Here, indeed, this great poet whose life as an artist began under the influence of writers like Pater and Villiers de l'Isle Adam, has removed himself from any trace of those influences. His rhythmic line is bare almost to austerity, but has all the nobility that such a bareness of outline can give. The mood of these poems, their particular lyrical impetus has changed from that of the lovely earlier verses : that impetus is perhaps, sharper, and darker, but in the later as in the early poems, the lovely sound and sense are fused into one as in no other lyrical poetry of our time. There is some kinship (though scarcely a physical resemblance) between certain of Mr. Yeats' earlier poems and certain of Shelley's lyrics—" A widow bird sat mourning on her bough," for instance ; but Mr. Yeats' individuality was never shadowed by the presence of any other poet. Such kinship as there was, lay in the peculiar impetus of the rhythmic line in both poets. But the melodic schemes were different. Writing of Shelley's lyrics in " The Pleasures of Poetry," Volume II, I said : " The actual variations of texture in the lyrics resemble, not so much the differences between silk and marble and stone, as the differences between the perfume of lily, dark rose, tuberose, violet and narcissus. These melodic effects are the result, in part, of his vowel-schemes, built up often on a foundation of two vowels only, or on a foundation in which each vowel is used both poignantly and dulled. But the beauty of the poems is often· as intangible as the scent of the flowers, and is not to be explained."

Mr. Yeats melodic schemes do not give us the feeling of the different perfumes of flowers. The vowel-schemes—so intensely fused with the rhythmic plan, or impetus, that they are indivisible, and appear to have been born into their form—not created by an outside handiwork—seem to have all the different variations of wind and of air, and it is a dew-laden, fresh wind or air, not one láden with perfume.

The strange wisdom that is radiant round such a poem as " Mohini Chaterjee " for instance, takes another form in the poem " Crazy Jane on God," in which the fusion of wisdom with the intensity

of passion is such that we feel the poem is a fire
rather than a form of words blown together.

> " That lover of a night
> Came when he would,
> Went in the dawning light
> Whether I would or no ;
> Men come, men go ;
> *All things remain in God.*
>
> Banners choke the sky ;
> Men-at-arms tread ;
> Armoured horses neigh
> Where the great battle was
> In the narrow pass :
> *All things remain in God.*
>
> Before their eyes a house
> That from childhood stood
> Uninhabited, ruinous,
> Suddenly lit up
> From door to top :
> *All things remain in God.*
>
> I had wild Jack for a lover,
> Though like a road
> That men pass over
> My body makes no moan
> But sings on :
> *All things remain in God.*"

In this poem the impression of those torn rags of
womanhood :

> " . . . a house
> That from childhood stood
> Uninhabited, ruinous,
> Suddenly lit up . . ."

is conveyed by the tuneless half-rhymes that appear
from time to time : " would-God " (a plunge into
immeasurable depths, this) in the first verse ; " sky-
neigh," " tread-God," " was-pass " in the second
verse ; " house-ruinous " (the extra syllable in the
second word gives a feeling of huddled misery),
" stood-God," " up-top " in the third ; " lover-
over," " road-God," " moan-on " in the fourth.
It is a memorable fact that the only pure rhymes
are in the first verse (where there is still the " would-
God " half rhyme on which I have commented
already) and this has much psychological significance.
In the second verse, there is a mixture of rising,
falling, and stretching half-rhymes or dissonances ;
in the third all are falling ; in the last verse, the
half-rhymes alternately fall and stretch wildly
onward into infinity. This is one of the deeply
significant technical interests of this great poem.

" Words for Music " indeed, from which the
foregoing and the following poem are taken, are, to
my feeling, undoubtedly the greatest lyrics of the
last hundred years, because of their intense fusion
of spirit and matter, because of their overwhelming
fire and their strange world-old wisdom, sung in
the voice of one who is impatient with " the loveless
dust."

CHAPTER IV

WILLIAM H. DAVIES

An unfortunate cold blast of wind blew poetry into fashion. The result has been that persons who have never known even a minor experience, criticize the truth of experiences felt through the heart, seen through the eyes, of men who were born to knowledge.

Mr. Davies' poems are among the beauties of nature, and are therefore disliked by persons to whom travelling in the country means a ride upon a motor bicycle.

These lyrics are exquisite as are those of Herrick, but they are on a rather larger scale and their loveliness, even when many images are used, is never of an artificial nature. Those images, indeed, are but reflections seen in a kingfisher's lake. Mr. Davies, to quote himself, is a " starer." He stares longer, and more intently, than starers who are not poets. He stares with more comprehension than most poets. And so he gives us the world as it is, but after it has been bathed in the radiance and the dew of a strange innocence.

The beauty of these poems is due mainly to their fresh and lovely fancy, and this is enhanced, often, by the shape, which is clear and rounded as an

apple, or has the soft perfection of a bullfinch's
rosy feathers. The beauty, indeed, lies more in
the exquisite images—those reflections in a lake,
in the roundness of the dew-clear apple—than in
the texture, which often has a kind of homely and
pleasing country roughness, like that of certain
leaves—raspberry leaves, for instance—or of cool
country sheets and of home-baked bread.

Yet in such a poem as " The Kingfisher," there
is an extraordinary beauty of texture as well as of
fancy and of shape :

" It was the Rainbow gave thee birth,
And left thee all her lovely hues ;
And, as her mother's name was Tears,
So runs it in my blood to choose
For haunts the lonely pools, and keep
In company with trees that weep.

Go you and, with such glorious hues,
Live with proud Peacocks in green parks ;
On lawns as smooth as shining glass,
Let every feather show its marks ;
Get thee on boughs and clap thy wings
Before the windows of proud kings.

Nay, lovely Bird, thou art not vain ;
Thou hast no proud, ambitious mind,
I also love a quiet place
That's green, away from all mankind ;
A lonely pool, and let a tree
Sigh with her bosom over me."

The poignance of the vowel-sounds in the first
lines give the lovely colour of the kingfisher's

feathers. The deep and changing vowels, the alliterative liquids, of

> " And *l*eft thee all her *l*ovely hues ; "

the change from the sound of " choose " to the deeper plunging sound of " haunts," and the change from the long clear O in " lonely " to the assonances " choose " and " pools " ; these sounds, echoing each other, or producing some clearer reflection of each other, seem like reflections in deep water. In :

> " I also love a quiet place "

we have a lovely secrecy, the sound of a gentle withdrawal into some green solitude, because of the shrinking vowels of " quiet " coming after the long dewy " qu."

The brightening of the sound in :

> " Go you and, with such glorious hues "

to the sharper clearer sound of " hues," produces again a reflection of the kingfisher's lovely flashing colours, seen in deep water.

This amazing visual beauty and clearness, as of something that has been washed in heavenly dews, is natural to all Mr. Davies' poetry. Take, for instance, these lines in a poem called " Charms " :

> " She walks as lightly as the fly
> Skates on the water in July."

The beauty and balance of this is due in part to the assonantal vowels of " lightly," " fly " and its rhyme " July," in part to the deeper dipping sound of " water " after the shining sound of

" skates," and in part to the assonance to " water "
—" walks."

A clear light and colour surrounds all these poems,
and often it cannot be explained, as with these lines :

" Ah, little girl with wool
What are you making now ?
Some stockings for a bird
To keep his legs from snow."

The juxtaposition of the idea of the clear feathers
of the bird and the white snow gives each a stranger
brightness.

How clear are the eyes that perceive these
beauties, how keen is their perception. To Mr.
Davies every flower holds the secret of Heaven,
and he stares at it with the knowledge of which
he has written in the following exquisite poem :

STARERS.

" The small birds peck at apples ripe,
And twice as big as them in size ;
The wind doth make the hedge's leaves
Shiver with joy, until it dies.
Young Gossamer is in the field ;
He holds the flowers with silver line—
They nod their heads as horses should.
And there are forty dappled kine
As fat as snails in deep, dark wells,
And just as shiny too—as they
Lie in a green field, motionless,
And every one now stares my way
I must become a starer too :
I stare at them as urchins can

When seamen talk, or any child
That sees by chance its first black man.
I stare at drops of rain that shine
Like glowworms, when the time is noon ;
I stare at little stars in Heaven,
That try to stare like the big Moon."

There are moments when, reading Mr. Davies,
we believe in reincarnation. The following poem,
we feel, must have been written by a poet living
in the same age as Herrick, yet there is nothing
derivative in manner or feeling. The poem has
been born of the poet's blood :

SMILES.

" I saw a black girl once,
    As black as winter's night ;
    Till through her parted lips
    There came a flood of light ;
    It was the milky way
    Across her face so black :
    Her two lips closed again,
    And night came back.

I see a maiden now,
    Fair as a summer's day ;
    Yet through her parted lips
    I see the milky way ;
    It makes the broad daylight
    In summer time look black :
    Her two lips close again,
    And night comes back.

How great is the contrast between this happiness
and such a poem as that I am about to quote.
Where could we find a more terrible simplicity,

than in the sound of this uncomplaining voice
coming from the depths, and, in its very un-
complainingness, loading our souls with guilt ?

The poem is called " The Heap of Rags."

" One night when I went down
 Thames' side, in London Town,
A heap of rags saw I,
 And sat me down close by.
That thing could shout and bawl,
 But showed no face at all ;
When any steamer passed
 And blew a loud shrill blast,
That heap of rags would sit
 And make a sound like it ;
When struck the clock's deep bell,
 It made those peals as well.
When winds did moan around,
 It mocked them with that sound ;
When all was quiet, it
 Fell into a strange fit ;
Would sigh, and moan and roar,
 It laughed, and blessed, and swore.
Yet that poor thing, I know,
 Had neither friend nor foe ;
Its blessing or its curse
 Made no one better or worse.
I left it in that place—
 The thing that showed no face,
Was it a man that had
 Suffered till he went mad ?
So many showers and not
 One rainbow in the lot ;

Too many bitter fears
To make a pearl from tears."

It is not possible to find a more poignant poem of the kind, or one more deeply experienced. If it is possible to hazard a criticism, however, I believe the poem would have been even finer without the last two lines :

" Too many bitter fears
To make a pearl from tears,"

which seem to reduce the poem in scale.

The same deep compassion and understanding shines in such poems as " Night Wanderers " with the terrible quatrain :

" Some of them laugh, half mad ; and some
All through the chilly night are dumb ;
Like poor, weak infants some converse,
And cough like giants, deep and hoarse."

Such lines as these, so heart-piercing and so true, shame the cold heart of the world. Mr. Davies almost invariably attains to an extraordinary compression, arriving at this largely by the means of a pure outline, and also by the simplicity which is one of the great beauties of his poetry. This simplicity, this compression, pure outline and poignancy, are particularly remarkable in such a poem as :

BODY AND SPIRIT.

" ' Who stands before me on the stairs :
Ah, is it you, my love ?
My candle-light burns through your arm,
And still thou dost not move ;
Thy body's dead, this is not you—
It is thy ghost my light burns through.

Thy spirit this : I leap the stairs,
To reach thy body's place ;
I kiss and kiss, and still there comes
No colour to thy face ;
I hug thee for one little breath—
For this is sleep, it is not death !

.   .   .   .   .

The first night she was in her grave,
And I looked in the glass,
I saw her sit upright in bed—
Without a sound it was ;
I saw her hand feel in the cloth,
To fetch a box of powder forth.

She sat and watched me all the while,
For fear I looked her way ;
I saw her powder cheek and chin,
Her fast corrupting clay ;
Then down my lady lay, and smiled—
She thought her beauty saved, poor child.

Now down the stairs I leap half-mad,
And up the street I start ;
I still can see her hand at work,
And oh, it breaks my heart :
All night behind my back I see
Her powdering, with her eyes on me."

It would, I think, be impossible to attain to a greater simplicity and poignancy than in this poem.

Mr. Davies with his poems reminds me of a bird-fowler. Indeed, once when I complained to him that a poem of my own was not working out as I wished, he said : " You sit quietly, and it will come. A poem is like a bird in a wood." He sits

G

quietly then, surrounded by all the birds of the wood, singing to him—or he wanders amongst the clearly seen beauties of Nature, looking at them with the eyes of the Happy Child, in his own poem—of a Blake-like innocence and radiance :

> " I saw this day sweet flowers grow thick—
> But not one like the child did pick.
>
> I heard the pack-hounds in green park—
> But no dog like the child heard bark.
>
> I heard this day bird after bird—
> But not one like the child has heard.
>
> A hundred butterflies saw I—
> But not one like the child saw fly.
>
> I saw the horses roll in grass—
> But no horse like the child saw pass.
>
> My world this day has lovely been—
> But not like what the child has seen."

This poem seems to me to have the clear colours of the world before sin was known, bathed in the light of a purer heaven than we can know.

In these days, when any clotted and incompetent nonsense is recklessly encouraged by the Press, as long as it is dressed in overalls and masquerades as a messenger of the new age, it is discouraging to find this great lyrical poet treated with a certain indifference. Whilst we have such a poet amongst us, we ought to honour him. But he has been consistently misunderstood and underrated from the first—simply because he is on traditional lines, and because his poems have a radiant innocence and a rare physical beauty.

CHAPTER V

T. S. ELIOT

In the year 1917, with the publication of Mr. Eliot's first volume, " Prufrock," began what may fairly be described as a new reign in poetry. The importance of the event cannot be exaggerated. The power of English poetry had been much weakened by such poets as Matthew Arnold and Dr. Bridges, who were interested equally in matter and in manner, but who had not regarded these as an indivisible entity, treating them, instead, as railway lines, running side by side for a considerable time, but bearing a different set of trains bound for different junctions. In other words, applicable both to the language and metres of these poems, that language, those metres, reproduced a certain effect of relationship, and a recognizable imitation, of the theme, but did not give us the reality. As Coleridge said in " Biographia Literaria," " The rules of the imagination are themselves the very powers of growth and production. The words, to which they are reducible, present only the outlines and external appearance of the fruit. A deceptive counterfeit of the superficial form and colours may be elaborated, but the marble peach feels cold and heavy, and children only put it to their mouths."

Matthew Arnold and Dr. Bridges produced a superabundance of marble peaches.

With Mr. Eliot, we were restored to a living world in poetry.

The title-poem of the first volume, " The Love Song of J. Alfred Prufrock," as well as certain of the other verses in this book, came, I am told, as a shock to persons clamouring for a cul-de-sac in the guise of tradition, but to informed traditionalists they should have presented no difficulty, since they are a logical development, transmitted to us through an intensely aware, acute, and inclusive consciousness, of methods used by Robert Browning in English and by Jules Laforgue in French. Nor was the influence of the Elizabethan dramatists lacking in Mr. Eliot's later work. Yet in none of the earlier or the later poems can we find anything stale, or seen through the eyes of another man. All is new and vital, and the muscular system of the verses arises from that of the poet, and is inherent in the needs of the poem. Mr. Eliot's poetry is a kind of ethereal body of the poet, as indeed, all great poetry must be.

Whilst we are on the subject of influences in poetry, it is interesting to note that Mr. Eliot, writing on the subject of logical development in technique, in his preface to Mr. Pound's poems, has said : " Poets may be divided into those who develop technique, those who imitate technique, and those who invent technique. When I say ' invent,' I should use inverted commas, for invention would be irreproachable if it were possible. Invention is wrong only because it is impossible ;

I mean that the difference between the 'development' and the 'sport' is, in poetry, a capital one.
There are two kinds of 'sports' in poetry, in the
floricultural sense. One is the imitation of development, and the other is the imitation of some idea of
originality. The former is commonplace, a waste
product of civilization. The latter is contrary to
life. The poem which is absolutely original is
absolutely bad ; it is, in the bad sense, 'subjective'
with no relation to the world to which it appeals.

"Originality, in other words, is by no means a
simple idea in the criticism of poetry.   True
originality is merely development."

In Mr. Eliot we have this true originality, and
the only relationship that his early work bears to
that of Browning is shown in his power of repro-
ducing the general state of the world mirrored in
one man, and in his use of ordinary speech rhythms ;
his relation to Laforgue in these early poems is
shown by a certain ironic disillusionment. Yet how
great, fundamentally, is the difference between the
powers of Mr. Eliot and those of the poets I have
mentioned. Laforgue, though intelligent and
subtle, had an invalid nervousness and self-
consciousness which is entirely absent from the work
of Mr. Eliot. Browning's capacity for emotion was
wide (though not deep) ; but the muscular system
of his verse was heavy and blunt ; bunches of
muscles show on the surface of his verse, like muscles
on the arm of a Strong Man at a Fair ; but we do
not see these muscles put to intelligent use.
Browning's verses straddle like a Strong Man ; Mr.
Eliot's verses moves like the Tyger burning bright ;

we can see the splendour of the muscles rippling under the fiery surface of the skin as the Tyger moves according to the needs of his nature, seeking the water pools.

Indeed, the flexibility of the muscular system, the complexity and subtlety of characterization, even in Mr. Eliot's earliest poems, cannot be compared with the coarser muscular system of Browning's poems. Mr. Eliot's rhythms flow, change, shift their focus, melt into other rhythms according to the needs of the subject, " adorning " (as Emerson would say) " nature with a new thing."

Note. —" It is not metres, but a metre-making argument, that makes a poem — a thought so passionate and alive that, like the spirit of a plant or an animal, it has an architecture of its own, and adorns nature with a new thing."—" Emerson : The Poet."

The architecture of Mr. Eliot's poems must be so described.

Let us take, for a minor instance among his earlier poetry, the opening lines of " The Love Song of J. Alfred Prufrock " :

" Let us go then, you and I,
When the evening is spread out against the sky
Like a patient etherised upon a table ;
Let us go, through certain half-deserted streets,
The muttering retreats
Of restless nights in one-night cheap hotels
And sawdust restaurants with oyster-shells :
Streets that follow like a tedious argument
Of insidious intent
To lead you to an overwhelming question . . .
Oh, do not ask, ' What is it ? '
Let us go and make our visit."

The fact that the first heavily accented word in the first line, is the word "go" gives a necessary touch of determination to this poem of indecision. The line " When the evening is spread out against the sky "—though it is actually of exactly the same length as the next line—both have a half-muted fraction of a syllable beyond their norm : ("evening," "table") bringing to mind the dumb softness of this half-light—appears to be slightly longer, more wearied, because of the mound we must surmount in the middle of " evening " (a mound caused by the extra half-syllable), whereas " table," though it begins with a flat stretch of sound, ends with the muted fraction of a syllable, falling away to nothingness.

In the fifth line :

" The muttering retreats "

owing to the shrunken length, that yet has a stretch of sound at the end, we feel that we are no longer in the open street that may lead anywhere ; we are, instead, behind the façade of a " one-night cheap hotel "—shut away, with the vague muttering sound of meaningless and unknown voices, from the living sounds of the streets.

In the next line :

" Of restless nights in one-night cheap hotels "

the growth of the memory of plural nights out of one night, the repetition that seems a haunting ghost more than an echo, this gives the sensation of the restless turning over and over of a sleepless body inhabited by a soul that is between sleep and awakening.

In this poem, then, we had already the beginning of that technical splendour, and superabundant vitality, that intense visual sense, conveying itself partly by means of rhythm, partly through the actual substance and texture of the verse, that we find in all Mr. Eliot's poems.

Amongst the other verse in this early volume, " Rhapsody on a Windy Night " appears to me to be just as interesting technically as " The Love Song of J. Alfred Prufrock." I have known an unskilled listener (by which I mean a listener unused to, or only half-educated as to, verse) to be misled on hearing this poem for the first time, misled by the *balance,* in spite of the constant change from the sober walking movement of some of the lines, into the running movement of other lines, now short, now long—into believing that these are not only sharply and closely rhymed *externally,* but, from time to time, *internally* also. This is the result of the extreme control in which the poem is held. Yet as a matter of fact, in the first verse, which consists of twelve lines, only the fourth and sixth, the ninth and twelfth lines, are rhymed, whilst in the seventh there are two internal rhymes, holding, as it were, the structure of the verse together.   In the next verse of ten lines, the short second and third lines, the almost motionless sixth and tenth, rhyme. But in the third verse, where :

> " The memory throws up high and dry
>   A crowd of twisted things ; "

there is no rhyme at all, for the memories consist of fragments.

These occasional rhymes, placed purposely at certain points in the poem, seem to gather together, within the region of one space of time, all these old memories of things seen and experienced, things which would otherwise lie scattered throughout space and throughout time. These rhymes, gathering together and enclosing these scattered things within our universe, occur by the laws of nature and not by a superimposed law.

Here, then, we have not only the beginning of Mr. Eliot's amazing genius for handling his material, but also the beginning of that power of creating a universe by making all time as one, by fusing all experience into one, after a long process of deliberate disintegration.

In an extremely interesting essay on the poems of Mr. Ezra Pound in *Hound and Horn* (Winter, 1931) the reviewer wrote : " The Cantos may be regarded as an epic of timelessness. That is to say, the poem represents Mr. Pound's endeavour to manage an arrest of time. Roughly, the method is that of identification, fusion of image."

If that is true of Mr. Pound, it is true in a higher degree of Mr. Eliot, who attains to a still purer identification and fusion, no matter how great the disorganization from which these are reformed.

Another example, too, of Mr. Eliot's power of attaining to an extraordinary compression and expressiveness, of conveying all the complexities of a character by means of fusing two widely opposed points of time—each throwing strong shadows of

their widely different significances—is shown in
these lines from the early poem " Mr. Apollinax " :

" When Mr. Apollinax visited the United States
His laughter tinkled among the tea cups.
I thought of Fragilion, that shy figure among the
birch-trees,
And of Priapus in the shrubbery
Gaping at the lady in the swing."

and in these :

" I heard the beat of centaur's hoofs over the
hard turf
As his dry and passionate talk devoured the
afternoon."

In these earlier poems, we have already one who
can ask :

" Would it have been worth while,
To have bitten off the matter with a smile,
To have squeezed the universe into a ball
To roll it toward some overwhelming question,
To say : ' I am Lazarus, come back from the dead,
Come back to tell you all, I shall tell you all.' "

But " biting off the matter with a smile " seemed
still, to this youth of genius, an easy matter ; he
was not yet the man who has " walked among the
lowest of the dead," and who has talked with angels.

It is interesting to notice that in the last line of
the above passage, as in the second line of :

" The muttering retreats
Of restless nights in one-night cheap hotels "

we have the foreshadowing of that sensation of

irrevocability, of a ghostly haunting, which Mr. Eliot produces by using the repetition, the echo of a phrase or a word, sometimes swirling round and back upon the original, sometimes rising like the wind or sinking like the wind as it dies, which we find afterwards in " The Waste Land."

> *Note.*—" Speak to me. Why do you never speak. Speak.
> What are you thinking of ? What thinking ?
> What ?
> I never know what you are thinking. Think."

In these early poems Mr. Eliot had already that intense identity which is one of the signs of a major poet. But it was only with the poems dated 1920, that the full flowering of his genius astonished the world.

That genius shows itself in the comprehensiveness, the hellish horror, the deep divination of these lines from " Burbank with a Baedeker, Bleistein with a Cigar " :

> " A lustreless protrusive eye
> Stares from the protozoic slime
> At a perspective of Canaletto.
> The smoky candle end of time
>
> Declines. . . ."

In these lines the impression of slime is given by the many slowing, dulling S's and the Z in the first two lines, and by the crawling movement of these. . . . " At a perspective of Canaletto " has the guttering movement of a candle that will soon die.

In this poem again we find those widely opposed contrasts which are part of Mr. Eliot's method. We have, too, though not in the lines I have quoted,

an appalling and terrifying laughter, apt, at times,
to change to that we may know where :

> ". . . breastless creatures under ground
>   Leaned backward with a lipless grin."

This laughter is heard in all the poems of this
period, excepting in " Gerontion "; and at moments
it masquerades as a human amusement. Who, for
instance, could resist the sheer fun of these lines
from " Burbank with a Baedeker, Bleistein with
a Cigar " :

> " Burbank crossed a little bridge
>   Descending at a small hotel ;
>   Princess Volupine arrived,
>   They were together, and he fell."

or these, from " Whispers of Immortality " :

> " The couched Brazilian jaguar
>   Compels the scampering marmoset
>   With subtle effluence of cat ;
>   Grishkin has a maisonnette ; "

and the passage which follows.

In " Sweeney Erect," however, we have the
" lipless grin " alone and a sound as of some laughter
heard in Hell. This hellish horror, this echo of
laughter, is heard even in the title " Sweeney
Erect " (with its black shadow :

> " Gesture of orang-outang
>   Rises from the sheets in steam.")

In this appalling vision of a brothel on the shore
of Hell, we have, for a breath of Heaven, only the
half-mocking cry :

" Display me Aeolus above
Reviewing the insurgent gales
Which tangle Ariadne's hair
And swell with haste the perjured sails."

but in the companion poem to this, amidst the
spiritual and physical horror of the company,
where man is part braying beast, part worm, part
ape, or where man is but the worm turned
vertebrate :

(" Apeneck Sweeney spreads his knees
Letting his arms hang down to laugh,
The zebra stripes along his jaw
Swelling to maculate giraffe.

.   .   .   .   .

The silent vertebrate in brown
Contracts and concentrates, withdraws ;
Rachel née Rabinovitch
Tears at the grapes with murderous paws ; ")

—in the midst of Hell, we find this despairing
beauty :

" The host with someone indistinct
Converses at the door apart,
The nightingales are singing near
The Convent of the Sacred Heart,

And sang within the bloody wood
When Agamemnon cried aloud,
And let their liquid siftings fall
To stain the stiff dishonoured shroud."

This, however, is obvious to every reader, and I
only reiterate these points for my own selfish

pleasure. We may remark, however, on the inspiration and genius that, in

> " Apeneck Sweeney spreads his knees
> Letting his arms hang down to laugh,"

uses, in the first line, minute sharp pin-points of vowels—like the beginning of a pin-point of brain—and, in the next, produces a gross sagging sensuality by the contrasted dark heavy vowels.

We meet Sweeney again, after a century of material experience compressed into the mechanism of thirteen years or so, in the sequence of two poems : " Sweeney Agonistes." But here he and his passive complements have lost the flapping laziness which characterized " Sweeney Erect " and " Sweeney Among the Nightingales " ; they seethe forward into an unknown future with a boneless movement, interweaving like worms intertwining. This movement continues throughout twenty pages, stopping only once, never hesitating otherwise excepting to change its gear from mood to mood, and even then never raising or lowering itself. The speed, the boneless movement merely seethes sideways or backwards.

The rhythms seem to be ordinary speech-rhythms, but the seething intertwining movements give them a world significance, which no ordinary speech-rhythms would hold. Mr. Eliot has, indeed, done with a terrifying perfection, exactly what all the youngest members of the new school of poetry have tried, and failed, to do. " Doris," whom we have met before, speaks with a gramophone imitation of a human voice, but her "terre-à-terre" friend who

bears the significant and horrible name of " Dusty "
has a voice which seems actually muffled by the
element of which she is a native.

In the second fragment, we have the attempt
of the debased rhythm of modern life to simplify
itself into the sound—not arising from, but lowered
from the needs of that life, of cannibal drums.

Sweeney :
                Yes, I'd eat you !
    In a nice little, white little, soft little, tender
        little,
    Juicy little, right little, missionary stew.
    You see this egg
    You see this egg
    Well that's life on a crocodile isle.
    There's no telephones
    There's no gramophones
    There's no motor cars
    No two-seaters, no six-seaters,
    No Citroën, no Rolls-Royce.
    Nothing to eat but the fruit as it grows.
    Nothing to see but the palm-trees one way
    And the sea the other way,
    Nothing to hear but the sound of the surf,
    Nothing at all but three things

Doris :
                What things ?

Sweeney :
        Birth, and copulation, and death.
    That's all, that's all, that's all, that's all,
    Birth, and copulation, and death.

Doris :

> I'd be bored.

Sweeney :

> You'd be bored.
> Birth, and copulation, and death.

Doris :

> I'd be bored.

Sweeney :

> You'd be bored.
> Birth, and copulation, and death.
> That's all the facts when you come to brass
>   tacks :
> Birth, and copulation, and death.
> I've been born, and once is enough.
> You don't remember, but I remember,
> Once is enough.

In this whole fragment, we have tne concentrated horror of this world reduced to the nakedness of this physical trinity, whose triumph is reiterated over and over again.

In the line :

" I've been born, and once is enough,"

we have the attitude of the world towards the spirit.

The rhythm of the earlier " Sweeney Erect " and " Sweeney Among the Nightingales," and that of " Whispers of Immortality " is roughly the same, inasmuch as all three poems consist of quatrains on the eight-syllable norm, and only the second and fourth lines of each quatrain rhyme ; but there is a significant difference. " Whispers of Immortality " has a certain appalling gallantry, for one thing. Owing to the regular gaps in the rhyme

scheme, the movement of each verse in all three of
these poems flaps lazily open, then flaps together
again, like rags of flesh or of bone blown away from
each other and then blown together again by the
empty will of the wind—blown backwards and
forwards, yet still adhering to the skeleton.

But in the Sweeney poems the movement seems
actually quicker and therefore more living (I have
not been able to discover the technical reason for
this) ; that movement comes *only* from outside ;
the characters, the objects, have no volition to
reorganize their human shape, whilst in " Whispers
of Immortality " there is a hopeless strength, a
hopeless persistence.

In " Sweeney Among the Nightingales," the
whole spiritual state of the characters is conveyed
by the actual sound of the first verse :

> " Apeneck Sweeney spreads his knees
> Letting his arms hang down to laugh,
> The zebra stripes along his jaw
> Swelling to maculate giraffe."

Here, after the first line, there is only hollowness,
blankness, lazy abysses of emptiness, stretches of
vacancy, contractions into shrunken nothingness,
and, amidst this, the hoarse animal sound of the A
in " jaw." All this is conveyed by the different
wave-lengths, the heights and depths of the A's
which run through the verse.

In " Whispers of Immortality," however, we
have a despairing attempt on the part of the
" lipless dead " to reorganize their shape, and this
is conveyed in the verse by an extremely subtle

H

system of alliteration and of echoes, which, at first, seems accidental.

" Webster was much possessed by death
   And [1]saw the [1]skull beneath the [1]skin ;
   And [2]breastless [4]creatures under [3]ground
   [4]Leaned [2]backward with a [4]lipless [3]grin.

   Daffodil [2]bulbs instead of [2]balls
   [1]Stared from the [1]sockets of the eyes !
   He knew that thought clings round dead [4]limbs
   Tightening its [4]lusts and [4]luxuries.

   Donne, I [1]suppose, was such another
   Who found no [1]substitute for [1]sense ;
   To [1]seize and clutch and [5]penetrate,
   [5]Expert beyond [5]experience,

   He knew the [6]anguish of the marrow
   The [6]ague of the skeleton ;
   No contact possible to flesh
   Allayed the fever of the bone."

The feeling of hopeless persistence is given, too, by the change from the soft S's to the S with a K inserted after.

Here we have agony in eternity, grown out of the pain of mortality ; and this is shown, in the last verse, by the gradually rising A sounds in the first two lines (the highest A echoing that of " penetrate " in the third quatrain) : " marrow," " ague."

This high sound sinks again, despairingly, to the echo of " anguish "—the word " contact " then rises again to the high phantom sound of " allayed " —an unreal balance tc the word " ague."   In this verse, then, as in " Sweeney Among the Nightingales " we have a scheme built up upon A sounds ; but the balance, and therefore the meaning, is utterly different.

A silly attempt has been made by a young critic, Mr. Alec Brown, in an essay on Mr. Eliot's poetry (*Scrutinies*, II, Wishart) to prove that the metre of " Gerontion " is fundamentally only an inflated version of the metre of the Sweeney poems. Under the spell of this nonsensical idea, he announces that " The characteristic of . . . Gerontion and the Sweeney poems is the persistence in the poet's mind of one metallic swinging, singing kind of metre ; the metre of the Sweeney poems, which crops out in 'Gerontion' too . . . let us note these prominent lines :

' In the juvescence of the year ' . . .

' Vacant shuttles weave the wind '

' An old man in a draughty house '

' The tiger springs in the New Year. . . .' "

" There are others too," he assures us, " that one feels to have been the same, but to have had their back broken by sticking in a word or taking one out.

A good example is :

' Beyond the circuit of the shuddering Bear '

which, without the ' shuddering ' is exactly of the type of :

' Cast in the unstilled Cyclades ! ' "

Insensibility could scarcely be carried further ! In the first place, the first accent of

" Beyond the circuit of the shuddering Bear "

is on the second syllable, whereas that of

" Cast in the unstilled Cyclades "

is on the first—and this fact gives the lines a completely different balance. Secondly, the two syllables of " unstilled " are of an equal length, and the movement seems to stretch outwards whereas the word " circuit " has a swirling movement. Even if we leave out the word " shuddering,"—a great impertinence to a poet of Mr. Eliot's supreme mastery over his medium—I can scarcely conceive of two lines grown on the eight-syllable norm which could bear less resemblance to each other. The only vague resemblance lies in the fact that both the mutilated line and the unmutilated have eight syllables. But the resemblance of one eight-syllabled verse and another eight-syllabled verse is as rudimentary as the resemblance of every kind of man with every other kind of man, and with each kind of ape ! No allowance is made for race, for colour, for movements, for habits, for mentality, for the different ways in which the soul works. As for the other discoveries made by Mr. Brown along these lines, " his blunders," to quote Swift's complaint about his servant Watt, " would bear a history." We are told that " In the juvescence of the year " resembles the rhythm of the Sweeney poems. Let us take the whole passage from which this phrase has been quoted, and then a passage from one of the Sweeney poems, and see if there is the faintest resemblance :

" Signs are taken for wonders. ' We would see a
      sign ! '
The word within a word, unable to speak a word,
Swaddled with darkness. In the juvescence of the
      year
Came Christ the tiger."

Compare this with the following passage from " Sweeney Erect " :

 (" The lengthened shadow of a man
     Is history, said Emerson
     Who had not seen the silhouette
     Of Sweeney straddled in the sun.")

Mr. Brown, in quoting " In the juvescence of the year " has mutilated the rhythm of the phrase, separating, or cutting into disjointed fragments a majestic and splendid passage which forms an indivisible whole, a living entity which grows inevitably from the swaddling darkness into the light.

In the line :

" Swaddled with darkness. In the juvescence of the
      year "

we have the rhythmical splendour of the march of the tiger. Mr. Brown has thrown the whole line out of gear—has thrown a heavy accent on the

word " In."   Mr. Brown quotes, as another example
of this " persistence in the poet's mind of one
metallic swinging kind of metre, the metre of the
Sweeney poems," " Vacant shuttles weave the
wind."   But Mr. Eliot wrote nothing of the kind.
He wrote, after the lines telling us about Fraulein
Von Kulp :

"Who turned in the hall, one hand on the door "

      " Vacant shuttles
Weave the wind.   I have no ghosts,
An old man in a draughty house,
Under a windy knob."

Has this young critic no feeling for the entity of
expressed rhythms, no feeling for the unexpressed
rhythms which lie in the blank spaces of a page ?
Before and after the slow " Vacant shuttles," the
wind flows blowing away memories, and bringing
others in their stead.   Yet Mr. Brown abolishes the
movement of these shuttles, and leaves no space
for the wind to blow in.

It would not be necessary to mention these new
readings, were it not that this great poet is, according
to my feeling, often misunderstood as to his implicit
meanings ;   and if, in addition, the intense
significance of his technique is to be distorted, then
meanings still more alien to the original will be
imputed to the poems, still further misunder-
standings will arise.

" Gerontion " is one of the greatest and most
significant of Mr. Eliot's poems, and though, for
once, I find myself in accordance with Dr. Leavis,
inasmuch as I am embarrassed for the fear of insulting

the reader's intelligence—I hope I shall be forgiven
for tracing a connection I believe to exist between
the opening of this, and the closing of " The Burial
of the Dead " in " The Waste Land." The author
has explained the main theme, both by means of the
title, and by the last two lines :
                    " Tenants of the house,
        Thoughts of a dry brain in a dry season "—
and these two lines make it, from one point of view,
unnecessary to examine the first page of the poem.
It may be for this reason, or it may be for the fear,
which I confess I share with Dr. Leavis, of " insulting
the intelligence of the reader " that critics have
avoided scrutinizing the implicit meanings which lie
under the surface of the first page. But it is possible to
be too afraid of pointing out the obvious. In the
opening lines of " Gerontion," then, I think we
have a version of the theme inspiring the lines :

" There I saw one I knew, and stopped him, crying
        Stetson !
    You who were with me in the ships at Mylæ ! "

Only in " Gerontion " we have one who was not
in the ships at Mylæ, or to whom that memory
is only now an outworn tale, being read aloud by
the voice of a boy who now means nothing to him—
the voice of his own lost youth.
" Here I am, an old man in a dry month,
    Being read to by a boy, waiting for rain.
    I was neither at the hot gates
    Nor fought in the warm rain
    Nor knee deep in the salt marsh, heaving a cutlass,
    Bitten by flies, fought."

The rain for which the old man is waiting has
the same significance as that of the water in " What
the Thunder said "—the last section of " The
Waste Land."
The lines :

> " I am an old man,
> A dull head among windy spaces,"

convey to us that the wind is but emptiness to
him, a dull loud noise, not the rushing of wind
in which come the Pentecostal Tongues.

In the lines :

> " My house is a decayed house,
> And the jew squats on the window sill, the
> owner,
> Spawned in some estaminet of Antwerp,
> Blistered in Brussels, patched and peeled in London
> The goat coughs at night in the field overhead ;
> Rocks, moss, stonecrop, iron, merds.
> The woman keeps the kitchen, makes tea,
> Sneezes at evening, poking the peevish gutter,"

we have a physical actuality ; but the meaning is
deeper than that. The two lines with which the
poem ends have told us what the word " house "
signifies in this connection :

> " Tenants of the house,
> Thoughts of a dry brain in a dry season."

Here, then, we are given not only physical
actuality, but also a spiritual meaning. The decayed
house, it is unnecessary to say, is the old man's

mind ; but it is not, perhaps, labouring the point
too much, if we suggest that the owner is Doubt,
in the person of the Jew, whilst the goat which
coughs overhead is a symbol of the physical lusts
of the body—enclosed now in a field where no
rain has fallen—where there is nothing but rocks,
moss, stonecrop, iron, merds. This last theme is
linked up with the woman who now is only the
maker of small household comforts—at evening
" poking the peevish gutter "—raking up old ends
and tags of time and outworn things. Then,
however, in the midst of all this deadness comes the
wonder, the splendour, the terror of the new life :

" Signs are taken for wonders. ' We would see a
        sign ! '
    The word within a word, unable to speak a word,
    Swaddled with darkness. In the juvescence of
        the year
    Came Christ the tiger

    In depraved May, dogwood and chestnut,
        flowering judas,
    To be eaten, to be divided, to be drunk
    Among whispers ; by Mr. Silvero
    With caressing hands, at Limoges
    Who walked all night in the next room ;

    By Hakagawa, bowing among the Titians ;
    By Madame de Tornquist, in the dark room
    Shifting the candles ; Fraulein von Kulp
    Who turned in the hall, one hand on the door."

Apart from the miraculously beautiful movement
of the lines about Christ the tiger, we must remark

how the Cæsura after " swaddled in darkness "
seems Darkness itself, out of which springs with a
tiger's leap, Light.

In this passage again, I take it that we are given
not only the physical actuality of Mr. Silvero,
Hakagawa, Madame de Tornquist, and Fraulein
von Kulp, but the supreme moments in the life
of their soul. Hakagawa's movement, is, perhaps,
not only that of a slavish subservience towards the
rich. Something from outside is forcing him to
bow his head in the presence of the ideal beauty.
Madame de Tornquist shifts the candles in the dark
room, seeking for more light. Fraulein von Kulp
turns in the hall, one hand on the door. But who
knows if that door leads to heaven or to hell !

Much has been written of the influences under
which Mr. Eliot has worked, of his poetical ancestry ;
and Dr. Leavis, in what any fair observer must
admit is a finely-reasoned passage in his essay on
Mr. Eliot (" New Bearings "), says : " The other
derivation he assigns to his verse " (the first was that
of Laforgue) " manifests itself plainly in the first
poem of the section following " Prufrock " that is
dated 1920. It is not for nothing that in " Gerontion " he alludes to one of the finest passages of
Middleton :

" I that was near your heart was removed therefrom
    To lose beauty in terror, terror in inquisition.
    I have lost my passion : why should I need to
        keep it
    Since what is kept must be adulterated ? "
                                    " Gerontion."

" I that am of your blood was taken from you
   For your better health ; look no more upon it,
   But cast it to the ground regardlessly.
Let the common sewer take it from distinction."

                    " The Changeling," V, III.

This is an interesting comparison, but I think
the likeness between the two passages, apart from
the fact that both have a superb muscular system,
is a rather superficial one. Both passages are the
outbursts of a despairing love, but the implicit
meanings are different. In Middleton, the blood,
though the common sewer will take it from distinction, is still anguished—it is still in the heart,
waiting to be spilt. But in " Gerontion " it is
spilt already :

" I have lost my passion : why should I need to
      keep it
   Since what is kept must be adulterated ? "

In this great poem we find the first foreshadowings
of the inclusive human consciousness of Tiresias in
" The Waste Land " :

" After such knowledge, what forgiveness ?   Think
      now
   History has many cunning passages, contrived
      corridors
   And issues, deceives with whispering ambitions,
   Guides us by vanities.   Think now
   She gives when our attention is distracted
   And what she gives, gives with such supple
      confusions
   That the giving famishes the craving.   Gives
      too late

What's not believed in, or if still believed,
In memory only, reconsidered passion. Gives
   too soon
Into weak hands, what's thought can be dispensed
   with
Till the refusal propogates a fear. Think
Neither fear nor courage saves us. Unnatural
   vices
Are fathered by our heroism. Virtues
Are forced upon us by our impudent crimes.
These tears are shaken from the wrath-bearing
   tree.

     .   .   .   .   .

The tiger springs in the new year. Us he devours.
       Think at last
We have not reached conclusion, when I
Stiffen in a rented house. . . ."

And the old man asks himself what is the sum,
what is the outcome of all human endeavour.
After the beauty, or the dirtiness of life, broken
wing-feathers, blown clean by the wind,

". . . De Bailhache, Fresca, Mrs. Cammel, whirled
  Beyond the circuit of the shuddering Bear
  In fractured atoms. Gull against the wind,
     in the windy straits
  Of Belle Isle, or running on the Horn,
  White feathers in the snow, the Gulf claims."

The names De Bailhache, Fresca, Mrs. Cammel,
have a strangely sordid sound, as of some international gang of drug-traffickers, or white-slave
traffickers and I imagine were chosen because of

the contrast of their dirtiness, with the splendour of "The tiger springs in the new year. Us he devours," much as the name "Stetson" was used in the great passage which ends: "The Burial of the Dead" in "The Waste Land," because of its intensely ordinary sound, which makes the contrast of the splendour, the wonder, the adventure in the ships at Mylæ more significant.

It is difficult for any watchful observer to understand how it was possible for Mr. Eliot's genius, his supreme power of fusing material and manner, not to have been recognized from the beginning, since this power of fusion is only to be found in major poetry. With the appearance of "The Waste Land," however, even the most reactionary or sleepy of critics become aware that in Mr. Eliot a new glory in English poetry had arisen.

The title of this poem, which made its first appearance in the opening numbers of *The Criterion* (October, 1922, and January, 1923), is taken from Miss J. L. Weston's book "From Ritual to Romance," the subject of which is the legend of the Grail. In this book the significance of the Waste Land is to be found in "Fertility Ritual." But in Mr. Eliot's Waste Land—in the Waste Land of our modern civilization—the old rhythms, uniting man with his brother-man, uniting man with woman in fruitful love, uniting mankind with the earth, these are destroyed, changed, or broken down. In the modern Waste Land the ground has, indeed, been ploughed up, but into furrows so deep they might be graves for all mankind. The seed is scattered—nor, where it has taken root, do the waters of the spirit come to refresh it. With the Machine Age, the natural rhythms of the soil and of the seasons have been broken up ; no longer have we a slow maturing of time, bringing our earth to harvest.

> "What are the roots that clutch, what branches
>   grow
>   Out of this stony rubbish ? Son of man,
>   You cannot say, or guess, for you know only
>   A heap of broken images, where the sun beats,"

The difficulty of blending this heap of broken images—images of today, images left from past civilizations and cultures—was very great. Mr. Eliot, therefore, with his supreme genius for organizing a poem, has used the symbols of the Tarot Pack (which has, as we know from " Ritual and Romance," a connection with Fertility Ritual, and is therefore peculiarly suitable for the purpose) as a means whereby he may sweep the " broken images " into such positions, such attitudes, that the shadows cast by them will fall into a pattern which forms a comprehensive and deeply significant whole. By this means, then, he has been able to draw together figures, symbols, and events, which would otherwise lie scattered throughout Time and Space, and has, at the same time, shown that these lie within the hand of an unescapable Destiny.

In the strange, muttering, half-alive whisper of the " clairvoyante " the whole scope of the poem is concentrated, made small for our inspection :

      . . . .   " Here, said she,
Is your card, the drowned Phœnician Sailor,
(Those are pearls that were his eyes.   Look !)
Here is Belladonna, the Lady of the Rocks,
The lady of situations.
Here is the man with three staves, and here the
      Wheel,
And here is the one-eyed merchant, and this card,
Which is blank, is something he carries on his back,
Which I am forbidden to see.   I do not find
The Hanged Man.   Fear death by water.
I see crowds of people, walking round in a ring."

The way in which the Cæsuras are cast, throughout
this passage, gives the impression that they are
lengthening shadows ; and, perhaps for this reason,
the clairvoyante's voice seems to be that of a sleep-
walker, wandering amongst the shadows, rather
than that of a sibyl amidst the desert lights of day.

The miraculous organization of the poem is
shown, not only in the use of the Tarot Pack as a
setting-off point, but in the way in which the
themes are repeated on all the different levels of
human consciousness and human experience, and
in such a manner that we do not realize, at first,
that we are not in a strange place—that we have
been there before, only the shadows lie differently—
that we are not listening to an unknown voice
speaking unknown words—for we have heard those
words before—only the voice is that of one who has
risen from the grave, or who, being dead, walks and
knows not that she is dead.

In " The Waste Land," the beauty, the radiance,

the deep and holy passion of the passage about the
hyacinth girl (the hyacinth is one of the flowers
associated with the sacrifice of the Slain God of
" The Golden Bough ") :

" ' You gave me hyacinths first a year ago ;
They called me the hyacinth girl.'
Yet when we came back, late, from the Hyacinth
    garden,
Your arms full, and your hair wet, I could not
Speak, and my eyes failed, I was neither
Living nor dead, and I knew nothing,
Looking into the heart of light, the silence."

will soon be changed to this terrible echo (in
" A Game of Chess ")

" ' My nerves are bad to-night. Yes, bad.   Stay
    with me.
Speak to me.   Why do you never speak.   Speak.
What are you thinking of ? What thinking ? What ?
I never know what you are thinking.   Think ! '

I think we are in rat's alley
Where the dead men lost their bones.

' What is that noise ? '
        The wind under the door.
' What is that noise now ? What is the wind doing ? '
        Nothing again nothing.
            ' Do
You know nothing ?   Do you see nothing ?   Do
    you remember
Nothing ? '

        I remember
Those are pearls that were his eyes.

' Are you alive, or not ? Is there nothing in
    your head ? ' "

In this passage, the actual hunting, haunting,
haunted, despairing movement of the wind rising
and falling, pausing and rushing onwards, is given
not only by the phrasing, the rushing sound, the
sudden sinking silence of the sentences, the rising
and falling of the rhythm, but also by the repetition
of a word, as in :

" Speak to me. Why do you never speak. Speak.
  What are you thinking of ? What thinking ?
      What ?
  I never know what you are thinking. Think."

In the whole passage, the only human voice
which is not part of the wind, sounds in the lines :

" I think we are in rat's alley
  Where the dead men lost their bones,"

and in those two lines rhythm is dead—it is not
even a broken thing dragging its weight along—
even the wind has lost its movement, and is scattered
like those bones.

In the rest of the passage, the weft left over from
the " empty shuttles of the wind " is mainly
composed of two threads, " do " and " nothing,"
and an echo of this floats towards us, drifting still
more aimlessly, with all the life gone out of the
wind, in the Fire Sermon :

" On Margate Sands.
  I can connect
  Nothing with nothing.

I

The broken fingernails of dirty hands.
My people humble people who expect
Nothing ! "

Here, then, we have an example of Mr. Eliot's
genius for organization. The poem, in reality,
presents but few difficulties, after many readings.
Yet we find a critic of acuity and insight, like Mr.
John Sparrow, professing himself unable to understand the passage which ends " The Burial of the
Dead." He tells us, in " Sense and Poetry " that
" this seems to be explicable only as the fruit of
personal association. The poet has described a
crowd in the city of London :

" There I saw one I knew, and stopped him,
    crying : ' Stetson !
You who were with me in the ships at Mylæ !
That corpse you planted last year in your garden,
Has it begun to sprout ? will it bloom this year ?
Or has the sudden frost disturbed its bed ?
Oh keep the Dog far hence, that's friend to men,
Or with his nails he'll dig it up again !
You ! hypocrite lecteur !—mon semblable—
    mon frère ! ' "

Commenting on this passage, Mr. Sparrow adds :
" Each of the sentences . . . is easy to understand,
each, in itself ' makes sense ' ; but why Mr. Eliot
should have addressed this particular series of
questions to Stetson, why he should record his
having done so at this point in the poem, what,
supposing he did so, Stetson can have made of
them—these are questions which it is impossible to
answer, nor is it any help to the reader to know that

one line is written in recollection of Webster and
another in recollection of Baudelaire. We are left
simply with the fact that to Mr. Eliot, with his
peculiar sensibility and his peculiar range of reading,
there presented itself this series of ideas, or a series
from which (for a reason which the selection does
not itself make apparent) he chose to preserve these
specimens. . . ." " These questions," says Mr.
Sparrow, " are impossible to answer." The only
difficulty actually lies in the fact that in this miracle
of poetry, so magical in its power of evoking the
deepest movements of the soul, so intensely poignant
—in these lines which are radiant with the light of
immortality, even amidst the dark anguish of
mortal pain—sense and language are one living,
suffering being, and cannot be separated without
destroying their life. Here we have reproduced a
great spiritual experience. The passage is not the
fruit of personal association, it is a universal
experience, and it is for *this* reason that Mr. Eliot
has chosen the name Stetson, which (just as the
names De Bailhache, Fresca, Mrs. Cammel, in
" Gerontion," evoke a stale memory of some foul
underworld) is a supremely ordinary name. Here,
then, is Stetson, an ordinary man with an ordinary
name—one of the crowd which

> " . . . flowed over London Bridge
> I had not thought death had undone so many."

But the great cry :

> " You who were with me in the ships at Mylæ,"

recalls to both these dead-in-life, the memory of

adventure and of battles amidst the great waters of the spirit.

The reason for the transition from the ships at Mylæ to :

> " That corpse you planted last year in your
>   garden,"

and the reason why these should appear in this particular part of the poem, are clear.   The corpse is at once the slain Vegetation God and our dead self—perished perhaps, in those far-away ships. It is also a buried memory :

(" You gave me hyacinths first a year ago . . .")
and the lines :

> " That corpse you planted last year in your garden,
>   Has it began to sprout ? will it bloom this year ?
>   Or has the sudden frost disturbed its bed ? "

picks up the theme of the lines with which the section begins :

" April is the cruellest month, breeding
  Lilacs out of the dead land, mixing
  Memory and desire, stirring
  Dull roots with spring rain.
  Winter kept us warm, covering
  Earth in forgetful snow, feeding
  A little life with dried tubers. "

The line :

" You ! hypocrite lecteur !—mon semblable—mon
      frère "

coming, as it does, after the anguished scream of

"Oh keep the Dog far hence, that's friend to men,
   Or with his nails he'll dig it up again,"

needs no explanation. But as it seems possible for
many readers to overlook the meaning of this whole
passage, it may not be unnecessary to point out that
it has two meanings, and one fixes the fact that the
experience is a universal one.

It is perhaps unnecessary to point out the terrible
travesty, perversion, complete reversal of the idea
of the primeval and holy fertility ritual, at the end
of "A Game of Chess," after the line :

"When Lil's husband got demobbed, I said."

In the very coarseness of the rhythm, in the
meaningless raucous sound of the vowels, we are
given the essence of these new savages, whose
savagery is no longer represented by a superb
muscular system. The human sacrifices of this new
benightment have not the heart torn out. Instead,
their flesh is stripped away, and we can almost see
the jerking of the nerves. Perhaps, in the sound
of some slum-cry, we shall learn the secret of why
the light seems a changed thing :

" ' Now Albert's coming back, make yourself a bit
    smart.
He'll want to know what you done with that
    money he gave you
To get yourself some teeth. He did, I was there.'

    .   .   .   .   .

' It's them pills I took, to bring it off,' she said.
(She's had five already, and nearly died of young
    George.)

'The chemist said it would be all right, but I've
never been the same.'
'You *are* a proper fool,' I said.
'Well, if Albert won't leave you alone, there it is,'
I said,
'What you get married for if you don't want
children.' "

In "The Fire Sermon" we are given an
impression of autumn mists by the varying length
of the stretches of the Cæsuras, and by the way
they are placed, in the first three lines :

"The river's tent is broken : / the last fingers of
leaf
Clutch and sink /1/2 into the wet bank. / ½ The
wind
Crosses the brown land, unheard. / The nymphs
are departed."

At the end of this great and impressive section,
after the piteous echo, floating so aimlessly, with all
the life gone out of the wind—of :

" On Margate Sands.
I can connect
Nothing with nothing.
The broken fingernails of dirty hands.
My people humble people who expect
Nothing,"

after the human experience, comes the sound of
all the voices of human desire fused into an eternal
flame, in the voice of the saint who has known the
fire of heaven and of hell.
At the beginning of the miraculous triumph of

technique fused with inspiration, " Death by
Water," we have a concentration of the themes :

> " Here, said she,
> Is your card, the drowned Phœnician Sailor,
> (Those are pearls that were his eyes.   Look !)
> Here is Belladonna, the Lady of the Rocks,"

and :

> " Stetson !
> You who were with me in the ships at Mylæ ! "

In this great poetry all experiences are as one,
in the wisdom, that has passed death, of the sailor
who has perished by the waters of the spirit.

In the first lines of the fifth section, " What the
Thunder Said," the anguish of those who have
watched beside the Hooded Man—the anguish of
the Forty Days in the Wilderness—the loneliness of
one who was soon to walk amongst thieves, the
anguish of both the unrepenting and the repenting,
are fused with the barren pains of the opening lines
of " The Waste Land."

> " After the torchlight red on sweaty faces
> After the frosty silence in the gardens
> After the agony in stony places
> The shouting and the crying
> Prison and palace and reverberation
> Of thunder of spring over distant mountains "

This gives us, in our *human* experience, the
" reverberation " of great primitive realities brought
into nothingness in this Waste Land (at the end of
" A Game of Chess ")—a reference to " That

corpse you planted last year in your garden,"
(" After the frosty silence in the gardens ") and a
reference to the agony of the painfully grown
living lilacs—symbols of the slain Vegetation God—
grown out of the Waste Land. This is fused with
the Forty Days in the Wilderness in " After the
agony of stony places." The reference, too, is to
the journey of the disciples to Emmaus. " The
shouting and the crying " we had at the end of
" A Game of Chess," in the terrible sounds blown
up, now and then, from the wastes of the streets.
The prison and palace we had also in " A Game
of Chess " and the

> " reverberation
> Of thunder of spring over distant mountains "

can need no explanation.

After the slow sinking of the phrase :

> " dying
> With a little patience "

we find ourselves once again circling vainly, but this
time slowly and with no life in our movements.
Rhythm has sunk into a dead thing, or a thing,
rather, which has lost its memory. The cry is
always for " water "—that water which could not
save, and the repetition of the word is, purposefully,
the only pulse-beat which could hold the sound
together. But by us, always, walks the Hooded
Man . . . who has been the Slain God of Frazer's
" The Golden Bough " in the beginning of men's
minds, and who is at once the Slain God and Jesus
Christ.

The splendour, the majesty, the fire and passion and control of the rest of the poem cannot be explained. The lines have a miraculous balance, floating upon the waves of passion, moving like flames. It is only possible to say of one detail, that anyone who has ever heard the thunder speaking in the mountains will know the accents of :

" Da
. . . . .
Datta
. . . . .
Dayadhvam
. . . . .
Damyata."

The sounds have the actual reverberations of the sound of the thunder echoing over mountains, and the Voice of God is embodied in form.

In " The Hollow Men," the terrible poem which succeeds " The Waste Land," with the epigraph from " The Heart of Darkness " " Mistah Kurtz—he dead "—we have another dirge for the world ; but this time we have not the voice of the nightingale.

(" The change of Philomel, by the barbarous king
So rudely forced ; yet there the nightingale
Filled all the desert with inviolable voice
And still she cried, and still the world pursues,
' Jug Jug ' to dirty ears.")

Nor have we the voice of the thunder. This is not a world in ruins, it is a world dissolving into nothingness. All the rhythms and pulses of life are dead, as we know from the whispering muscleless half-movements of the first section. This is

conveyed above all by the use of repetitions instead
of rhymes twice in the first verse, and by the use,
for a rhyme, of grass and glass—a rhyme where only
one letter is changed.　This technical genius conveys
the failure of active life.　Indeed, in the first two
sections, the only trace of movement—and how small
it is—lies in the line :

"Rat's coat, crowskin, crossed staves"

and this is because of the hard C's, the hard K,
and the dry T's placed near together.

In the fifth section, however, the broken springs
make a temporary spurt, only to break at the end
of each line, excepting in the hopeless round of :
"Here we go round the prickly pear," and the
three succeeding and repetitive lines, and in the
appalling last verse.

The next three poems, published separately in
the Ariel Series, are very different to "The Hollow
Men" in mood and in technique ; these poems,
which are concerned with religion, show no breakdown of rhythm, but a giving-up of the will.　I
do not know how to express it otherwise.　This,
then, seeming inertness is a purposeful one.

The change from these poems to "Ash
Wednesday" is significant.　In the first section, we
are given by means of the repetition of half-
sentences, and of whole sentences, and by means of
new fragments of sentences, the weariness of him
who is ascending the stair, and the humility.

No longer, as in "The Journey of the Magi," is
it said :

"I should be glad of another death"

no longer, as in " A Song for Simeon," is it said :

" I am tired with my own life and the lives of those after me."

Here instead, is a prayer for patience in :

" . . . the time of tension between dying and birth."

It is a poem of the greatest technical interest and subtlety ; it is also one which has been held to present many difficulties and obscurities. Who, it is enquired, is the Lady, and what do the three white panthers signify ? The Lady may, or may not, be a figure of religious meditation, part of that life which has cried :

" Consequently I rejoice, having to construct something
Upon which to rejoice,"

and part of the garden where :

" . . . the fountain sprang up and the bird sang down."

The three white leopards should need no explanation. They are part of the scaffolding of the poem. In the third section of the work, we have that climbing of the stairs whose movement we felt in the beginning of the first section—a movement of one who does " not hope to turn again "—the " strength beyond hope and despair " which characterizes the whole poem.

" Ash Wednesday " was followed by the superb " Triumphal March," published separately in the Ariel Series. And in this great poem we have as I see it, the presentation of the poor world that is waiting for the coming of Christ—for the great coming; and that is given, in His stead, Cæsar, the king of the world.

> "So many waiting, how many waiting? what did
>   it matter, on such a day?"

and then the terrible march onward, in place of Him, of

> "5,800,000 rifles and carbines,
>   102,000 machine guns,
>   28,000 trench mortars,
>   53,000 field and heavy guns,
>   I cannot tell how many projectiles, mines and
>   fuses,
>   13,000 aeroplanes,
>   24,000 aeroplane engines,
>   50,000 ammunition wagons,
> now 55,000 army wagons,
>   11,000 field kitchens,
>   1,150 field bakeries.

> What a time that took. Will it be he now? No."

But now at last he comes—but

> "There is no interrogation in those eyes."

Then comes the cry, which we find in all the poems of this great poet—though taking many disguises, sounding through many voices:

>   . . . "Please, will you
>   Give us a light?
>   Light
>   Light."

CHAPTER VI

SACHEVERELL SITWELL

GREAT is the confusion as to the needs of poetry in this age, and this confusion arises from a muddle-headed conception, on the part of certain critics, that a poem is of no importance unless it voices some purely contemporary feeling or problem, or produces a photographic representation of some contemporary theme. The only necessity in poetry, it appears, is this : that it should not be created as a work of art.

The world in which poetry is allowed to live is becoming narrower every day, though it is not necessary to attach any importance to Dr. F. R. Leavis' announcement that " It does not seem likely that it will ever again be possible for a distinguished mind to be formed, as Mr. Powy's has been, on the rhythms sanctioned by nature and time, of rural culture."

The present writer is not advocating a schism between life and poetry, but only that the aims and themes of poetry should not be limited so drastically. It is time that we readmitted what is known as pure poetry. The average reader, bewildered by the irresponsible statements, founded on a little knowledge and no sensibility, made by certain critics, will now accept any loosely knit conglomeration of unilluminated and unassimilated statements, as great poetry. It may be said with truth that it would be impossible to find a poet who has been more foolishly underrated than Mr. Sitwell, and for reasons that have no connection whatever with poetry. Mr. Allen Tate, writing some time ago in *The New Republic* on the subject of Milton (October 21st, 1931) explained that when we read poetry we bring to it the pseudo-scientific habit of mind ; we are used to connecting things up in vague disconnected processes in terms that are abstract and thin, and so our sensuous enjoyment is confined to the immediate field of sensation." In most cases, when we read the work of the newest school of poetry, no sensuous enjoyment is felt, for it inhabits a blind and unsensed world. But it is exactly this belief that poetry should be only a pseudo-philosophy expounding pseudo-scientific ideas, that has prevented Mr. Sitwell, whose poetry communicates an intense and wide sensuous enjoyment, from being recognized by the less intelligent readers of poetry as a magnificent poet.

The late Professor Saintsbury suggested that we are in need of " a test to decide whether a man cares for poetry as poetry, or whether he cares for it as expressing some sentiment, or conveying some meaning, which is agreeable or seems respectable to him." Let us, then, cast aside our respectability for a while, and examine the poetry of Mr. Sitwell.

It has been brought as a charge against this poet that he is in the habit of

" Annihilating all that's made
  To a green thought in a green shade."
but as a matter of fact, he does nothing of the
kind. All he does, is to remove himself from the

" Rattle shuffle ; Rattle : shuffle ;
  The train's coming quickly
  Coming
  LOUDLY
  Rattle shuffle rattle shuffle
  STOP."

school of poetry; not, strangely enough, because his
technique is inadequate, nor because his creative
power is insufficient, but because their verse is
silly, inexpressive in manner and dull in theme.

Mr. Sitwell's world is very far away from the
blind and unsensed world which we shall examine
in the last chapter of this book. His is a world
where nearly every sensory impression (and his
senses are peculiarly acute) conveys a spiritual
impression, is a means by which he may read the
meanings of that other world of which this physical
world is the covering.

The texture, though not the structure, of Mr.
Sitwell's verse bears a considerable resemblance
when it is sunny, though not when it is shady,
mournful or poignant, to the texture used by Blake
in " How Sweet I Roamed " and the sunny part
of " The Book of Thel." His use of sibilants and
liquids, his vowel-technique, his sense of the use
to be made of the different wave-lengths of the
changing and shifting vowels (as, for instance, his

handling of the difference between the length of
the sharp I and the dulled I), these are incredibly
subtle. Writing of a certain vowel scheme in
" Lycidas " (in the " Pleasures of Poetry," Vol. I)
I said " Certain blind people are enabled, by their
deprivation of a later sense than that of feeling—
sight—to know whether it is night or day simply
by the sensation of the different lights upon their
skin. This vowel scheme appears to me to show
the same sensibility." This applies, also, to Mr.
Sitwell's acute sensibility to texture, his complete
understanding of vowel schemes. " Melody," said
Beethoven, " is the sensual life of poetry. Do not
the spiritual contents of a poem become sensual
life through melody." This sensual life, this
melody, are gained not only by the melodic line,
but also by the cunning use of vowels, although,
as a rule, without the learned and instinctive use
of consonants, sharpness of outline is lacking. It
cannot be denied that certain vowels, used in a
certain way, not only alter the actual surface of a
line, but actually widen and stretch it. These,
and the cunning use of liquids, give, too, the faintest
and most subtle pauses, the feeling of a faint breath
of air blowing between the words. Mr. Sitwell
possesses this cunning so that, at times, his texture
is soft as the dewy bosom of a bird, floating from
sunny spaces among soft warm dark leaves, or it is
deep as the shadow cast by faunal branches weighted
with dew.

It will be best, for the purpose of explaining these
matters, if we turn first to " Doctor Donne and
Gargantua," which is Mr. Sitwell's longest poem.

The theme of this work is, to quote the author's preface, " a contest between good and evil, between the spiritual and the physical." It is, in short, the fight against God, and " God's lonely game." As Gargantua says :

" Donne's to snare a meteor wet and wild,
   And I'm to get a mandrake root with child :
   Both of these are games that we are at with God."

In this poem :

" God whom you worship, and the other Gods of
      other men :—
   Take yours, for instance :—plays a lonely game
   Moving his pawns, in armies, on each other ;
   The Knights riding by loud light of stars over the
      field,
   Themselves like sunlight flashing between shades,
   As they go from dark to light over woods and
      plain."

In this lovely passage the texture is one with the theme, was born from it. That enchanted feeling of a world of deep-grassed dew-wet fields on a summer night, was conveyed by the echoing of the long I's, which lengthen the line, and by the two L's placed close together ; " loud " being a long stretch of cool sound, like a field of deep grasses cool with dew and shining in the light of the great stars ; " light " being slightly less long than " loud," but higher—like a sound floating in the air. These L's find faint echoes *inside* the last word of that line, " field " and in several words of the next line :

" themselves like sunlight flashing between shades,"

J

Then the echoes fade, and are gone.

The theme, then, of this strange poem which cries of " the two shadow worlds, the real and metaphysical," is the battle against God from a universe that man has changed to a world of chance and doom—the attempt to conquer Fate by means of taming the elemental forces and the forces of nature into an unnatural servitude to man. The two worlds, the real and metaphysical, of which Gargantua and Donne are the protagonists, have become brothers ; they march side by side in their endless and hopeless battle, meeting endlessly but unwittingly the Third Protagonist, who watches, waits, beneath a myriad disguises.

In the following two passages (they are not, however, amongst the most successful poetry that Mr. Sitwell has written, and I quote them only because they explain the theme) Gargantua, " that form of smoke in leather armour of his own thick hide," tells us of the two campaigns that shall set free mankind :

" The way in which I'm certain that our safety lies
　Is to order, as we will, the very substance of our
　　race :
　We'll take an antidote against our poison
　And kill our human weakness by an alien strength ;
　By this means. The mandrake, most deadly of
　　the race of plants,
　If we could only join ourselves by bonds of
　　friendship,
　Cancelling its enmity, that we need never fear
　　it more,

From poison will be turned to balm.
Born of this union the future race
Are half immortal, free from poison's bane,
By this much stronger for their fight with God."

On the other hand :

" The meteor, now, for instance, what would our
        gain be ?
It would warn him of our power and make us
        independent.
The handful of metal that a meteor melts to,
When it falls upon the earth or plunges deep
        into the sea,
Will form our elixir and work our wonders.
Not only is our meteor a private gold mine ;
It cures all illnesses, and more important far
The feathers that we fly with to another star
Are woven of those golden wires that shine."

On this occasion, Mr. Sitwell's sense of texture
has deserted him, and I have quoted these lines
only because they at once explain the theme, and
exhibit Mr. Sitwell's worst danger—that of suddenly
changing the scale, dwarfing it by the means of
smaller imagery.

Now let us examine the following strange, dark,
haunted and echoing lines, in which God, contemplating His own lonely game, thinks of other of
His pawns : " My Cæsar and Pompey of these
later shadows."

" Pompey is an arrogant high hollow fateful rider
In noisy triumph to the trumpet's mouth,
Doomed to a clown's death, laughing into old age,
Never pricked by Brutus in the statue's shade."

In this passage, the " high hollow fateful rider "
is brought before us by the texture of the two first
lines ; the " hollowness " is conveyed by the empty
breath of the aspirates placed close together in
" high hollow," by the dark sound of " hollow "
and its higher dissonance " noisy," and its still
higher dissonance " mouth " (though none of these
sounds are really high), and by that long terrible
trumpet sound of " doomed." The preordained
movements of the " high hollow fateful rider " are
shown us by the tossing up and down in the first
line, caused by the different wave-lengths of the
vowels, by the different degrees of depth and
height, of the vowel sounds.

A very strange effect is caused by the assonances
ending the lines :

" Doomed to a clown's death, laughing into old age,
Never pricked by Brutus in the statue's shade."

In the change from the sound of " age "—a sound
which has body, but which seems crumbling and
shrinking into dust (perhaps because of the faint
shrinking shadow thrown by the " ge " coming
after the long A), in the change from this to the
slightly longer and flatter sound of " shade," with
its menacing, shuddering beginning (actually
" shade " is a kind of reversed shadow of " age,"
a shadow falling backwards, since the " sh " is a
sort of flatter echo of the " ge "), in this change,
preceded by the far shorter A of " statue," less
long, less real, than the lengthening shadow that is
thrown by it, we have the change from the crumbling

physical world to that world of untouchable reality which lies about us.

One almost infallible way of testing the worth of poetry is to place it in juxtaposition to a poem of the same kind, or purporting to be of the same kind, by another author. We will therefore compare the above passage from Mr. Sitwell with a passage from a poem that has been " enthroned " by Mr. and Mrs. Grigson in their paper *New Verse*. I will not give the name of the author, but Mr. Grigson, who has not only " dethroned " the unfortunate but oblivious Mr. Sitwell, but has also, metaphorically speaking, pelted him with all the treasures to be gathered in the dustbins of Keats Grove, Hampstead, has, I imagine, " enthroned " the writer whose verse I shall quote, because he is the herald of the new poetry of which I understand we are so much in need. This masterpiece—it is entitled, simply and modestly, " Poem "—is in four parts, and here are the last two :

III

" Which is the world ? of my two sleepings, which
    Shall fall awake when cures and their itch
    Raise up this red-eyed earth ?
    Pack off the shapes of daylight and their starch,
    The sunny gentleman, the welshing rich,
    Or drive the night-geared forth.

    The photograph is married to the eye,
    Grafts on its bride one-sided skins of truth ;
    The dream has sucked the sleeper of his faith
    That shrouded men might marrow as they fly."

IV

" This is the world ; the lying likeness of
Our strips of stuff that tatter as we move
Loving and being loth ;
The dream that kicks the buried from their sack
And lets their trash be honoured as the quick
This is the world.   Have faith.

For we shall be a shouter like the cock,
Blowing the old dead back ; our shots shall
        smack
The image from the plates.
And we shall be fit fellows for a life,
And who remain shall flower as they love,
Praise to our faring hearts."

An appalling affair ! Metaphysics have not helped
here. The idea is really of no importance, and
the thick squelching, cloying, muddy substance of
the   " which,"   " itch,"   " shapes,"   " starch,"
" welshing rich " verse, and the equally, or almost
equally hideous " kicks," " sack," " trash," " quick,"
" cock," " back," " smack," affair—these defeat
criticism.   In muddiness and incapacity, they leave
T. E. Brown's " God wot plot " arrangement at
the starting post.

We will, I think, return to Mr. Sitwell. His
poetry, made of " the two-shadow worlds, the real
and metaphysical," marching together in a universe
of ghosts, has a strange fourth-dimensional quality.
The small everyday incidents of life loom out of
their temporal world of shadow (soon to be changed,

soon to be melted into other temporal movements)
into a world of reality, then they melt again and
are gone. The tangible ordinary objects of an
ordinary world become symbols of the waiting,
watching world that lies about us—they assume
the quality, the radiance, of immortality, then they
fade before our eyes. Even the tennis balls with
which the Knights and Ladies of the Abbey of
Thelema are playing, these seem nothing but the
balls of snow, they melt and are gone with the
summer day and its glamour.

> " This summer day the spheres of hazard
>   Are talismans of snow, let us suppose."

.   .   .   .   .

> " Such is the sensual world, of melting, or
>   enduring,
>   And I hold it next the other one, sharp war
>   of the spirit,
>   Fighting for nothing, with no token won, or lost,
>   Out of endless battles, in deserts, and heaped
>   cold,
>   The very fuel of winter.
>   You can choose between these hazards, or
>   salvations ;
>   Stabbed Cæsar and dead Pompey are ghosts in
>   hollow porches
>   Inviting you to enter,
>   They guard the brothel doors but not to stop
>   you entering.
>   In long winter, when dark day is night,
>   Since the roofs of Thelema on a slant for snow

Are steep in that pale thatch,
The eaves of slant moonlight dipped into the
    day,
We will march our heraldry from courts of
    hazard
And melt it a red fire, at a hecatomb of fir-cones,
That burn their quills of resin for our flames
    of legend ;
There does Gargantua, on this crater-edge of
    firelight,
Build the embers into towers and caves,
For this is his winter-war in wiles of talk,
While my other hero in these goose-plumed
    days
Plots at his table with quill pen and paper.
The courts with feather-litter of the cold are
    filled
And the dead woods hear no hunting-horn,
But drop, now and then, their burdens in one
    footfall ;
These evening legends to dark pits of ghosts
Grow in Gargantua's parallels to the cold,
For he matches the winter with its raps on
    door and window,
By iron-mail on the winding stair
And a white horse at barred windows that no
    hand dare open.

Here do I leave them for a night of noises,
My Tarzan, my ape-man, whom I'll make again,
And the old philosopher in his cell of books ;
We will leave them at the fireside till we break
    into their legends

And knock the red logs into a light to show
    their faces.
Yes ! stay there !
Except we move you, up dark stairways,
For your night in the black pit of ghosts,
Till I wake you with a fanfare and you take
    your places,
Just where we leave you, at red towers and
    caves."

.   .   .   .   .

How strange and perfect is the arrangement of
the snow-soft f's, i's, and ea's of :

" The courts with feather-litter of the cold are
    filled "

(" feather," " litter " and " filled " being drifting,
almost soundless, echoes of each other, some faintly
longer and colder than others) followed by the dark
mournfulness of the sound in :

" And the dead woods hear no hunting-horn."

The last line has the same darkness, depth and
subtlety as Milton's lines :

" Yet once more, O ye laurels, and once more
    Ye myrtles brown with ivy never sere."

A dark and mournful air moves through all these
strange lines, so full of long shadows, so full of
lengthening echoes dying away into a silence that
is like music.

Note.—I hope that the use of the expression " echoes " will not be
made an excuse for insulting Mr. Sitwell by saying that his poetry is
an echo of the poetry of the past. Mr. Sitwell is a poet on great
traditional lines, but his poetry is his own, and he echoes no man.

I would ask the reader to compare, for a moment, the passage in question with the following lines, describing also a winter evening and a fireside, since, as I said before, only by comparing two poems or parts of poems on the same subject, can we arrive with any justice at a decision as to the merits of a poem. It will not be out of place to remind the reader that the author of the poem from which I am about to quote is one of the most extravagantly praised of the younger poets—(I do not give his name because some of his work shows a certain promise and I do not want to be discourteous to him)—whilst the appearance of any collection of poems by Mr. Sitwell is the signal for an outburst of noisy abuse on the one hand, and of complete neglect on the other.

" Taller to-day, we remember similar evenings,
    Walking together in the windless orchard
    Where the brook runs over the gravel, far from
        the glacier.
    Again in the room with the sofa hiding the
        grate,
    Looking down to the river when the rain is over,
    See him turn to the window, hearing our last
    Of Captain Ferguson.
    It is seen how excellent hands have turned to
        commonness.
    One staring too long, went blind in a tower,
    One sold all his manors to fight, broke through,
        and faltered."   etc.

We shall be told, as usual, that this is a fragment of real life (because life is boring and this fragment

is boring), whereas Mr. Sitwell's is an unreal world.
But is this so ?   Is not the passage from the unnamed poet merely the flatly-written and unliving
record of an unlived and undigested incident ?   Is
not the passage quoted from Mr. Sitwell an assimilated and transmuted experience recorded in
inevitable poetry in which the texture and the
shape are born from the theme ?   And in any case,
which of these two fragments is the more beautiful
in sound, which is the more subtle in vision, which
evokes the deepest memory of actual life as well as
of the life of a dream ?   Which more increases our
experience ?   Which gives us the more delight ?

Leaving the world of winter shadow for Mr.
Sitwell's " green thought in a green shade," we
may examine the lines which open the second
canto of " Doctor Donne and Gargantua " :

" Such are the clouds—
 They float with white coolness and snowy shade,
 Sometimes preening their flightless feathers.
 Float, proud swans, on the calm lake
 And wave your clipped wings in the azure air,
 Then arch your neck and look into the deep for
   pearls,
 Now can you drink dew from tall trees and sloping
   fields of Heaven,
 Gather new coolness for to-morrow's heat
 And sleep through the soft night with folded
   wing !
 Ride still at anchor, high above Thelema,
 While the gardener goes down the long ladders
   of rain,

Planting new flowers, to train
Darker shadows to grow round the windows
For serenades answered from darkness to darkness,
Set free with a whirr of wings,
From out their cage of strings."

The lovely floating movement of the first nine lines is not due only to the fluctuations, the flowing forward and backward of the varying lengths of the lines. We feel, actually, a faint air wandering from time to time, between, under, and above, certain of the words ; and this is due to the exquisite and incredibly subtle pauses (which are not only of varying lengths but of varying depths), resulting from the different wave-lengths of the vowels, and, as well, from the use of liquids and sibilants. Especially do we find this air wandering in the line :

" Sometimes preening their flightless feathers "

and in this :

" And sleep through the soft night with folded
    wing ! "

In these lines, there is the faintest slowing of the movement, due to the long I and the E's ; it is due, also, to the soft alliterative F's in the first line, with the lengthening liquid L. In the second line the effect is due not only to the vowel-scheme I have mentioned, but to the " d " of " fold," the " ft " of " soft " followed by the " t " which ends " night " and echoes the " t " of " soft."

These lines appear to me to be a miracle of technique, the result of inspiration absolutely controlled, in which the texture and the movement

are born of, and cannot be separated from, the
meaning.

After the transitional line :

" Ride still at anchor, high above Thelema "

and the slow melting beauty of :

" While the gardener goes down the long ladders
    of rain,"

the sound is sharper, the texture has a dew-sharp
echoing glitter like that of dark leaves that are
laden with dew and the light of summer. This
alternates with a deeper, warmer, softer darkness,
like that of the leaves and the smell of an orange
or lemon grove. These effects are gained partly
by the use of sharp glittering " tr's " and less sharp,
but still echoing " r's," and by the round dew-wet
sound of " planting "—partly by the sudden appearance of two rhymed couplets, and by the fact that
while in the first of these couplets the second line
is considerably shorter than the first, in the second
couplet both lines are almost equally short, though
the first line has an unaccented syllable more than
the second. But that syllable is so unaccented that
it seems to run, or to flutter like the birds moving
among the soft dark branches. These couplets and
especially the second, give freshness and crispness.

In the line :

" Planting new flowers, to train,"

after the word " flowers " with its faint flutter, its
little shadow, comes a long cool breath of air, a
pause, giving balance to the line. This arises from
the fact that " flowers " is a word of one and a

quarter syllables. Dr. Bridges, when writing of Milton's blank verse, and his system of elisions, explained that W may be disregarded as a vowel; as in the words " power," " bower," " flower," " shower," etc. This, as I said in the introduction to the first volume of my " Pleasures of Poetry," is only an excuse for introducing a line which is longer than other lines because of its lengthening shadows; since " flower " and " shower," etc., are words not of one syllable with an elided, muffled or dead syllable added, but of one and a .quarter syllables. In other words, that extra fraction of a syllable throws a little shadow, gives the faintest movement—but definitely a movement—exactly like that which a leafy, flowery bough, weighed with dew, gives when it trembles with dew and the dew falls.

Again, in the lovely passage quoted below, we find ourselves in a leafy world; but this time it is a world where the branches are wild and satyrine, and not like those of the warm gardens we have just left.

" Midday, the sloped watershed of light,

Parts the morning, the long faunal hours

Stay talking in the woods, for now one hears

Clang of sword and trumpet from the hard leaves

Hitting out, loud glittering, in the sharp falling
    light

Spilled like thrown water."

Note.—I have marked the groups of assonances and dissonances with numbers, according to their grouping.

In the lovely texture of this we find the difference
between the shadows cast by heavy still leaves, and
that cast by hard sharp glittering leaves, shadows
falling in dew-chilled bird-haunted air. This is
the result of the dark dissonances (so faint, so subtle,
they might almost be assonances) of " watershed,"
" morning,"   " faunal,"   " talking,"   " sword,"
" falling "—all varying with incredible slightness and
subtlety in depth, warmth, or chilliness. We find
ourselves lifted into light at the end of the third
line, by the word " hears " (with its faint echo
sounding among the leaves, which is the result of
the word having one and a fraction syllables)
coming after the darker dissonance " hours " which
ended the last line. This is followed by the sharp
dew-shining shape of bright leaves, conveyed by
the sound of " Hitting out, loud glittering " with
the echoes of " hitting " and " glittering " (the
second word having in the middle, a half elided syllable which causes a slight flutter, like that of a bird
dashing through sharp leaves), and, in the next line,
their assonance " spilled "—a word which seems to
have a long dew-chilled space in the middle, caused
by the liquid Ll's. These echoes surround the
still more subtle echoes of " out " and " loud,"
the second word " loud " being longer than " out "
because of the " d " that ends it, so that we feel
we are hearing echoes sounding down some long
vista cut between the trees.
Throughout Cantos II and III of this poem,
the strange airy and wandering differences in the
movement, perfectly controlled, but seeming there
by the laws of nature (as, indeed, they are) these

movements, fluctuating, flowing forward, changing because of the differences in the texture, and the inevitable growth, quickening or slowing, of the rhythm (this being the result partly of structure, partly of texture), these give us again the change from rich sun to richer shade, the difference between the dewy morning splendour of the sunlit spaces, and the shadows cast by dark and glittering leaves, or by young sharp leaves, the ecstasies of the differences between summer air and the summer breath of wind, between the secrecy of dew falling and the poignancy of the first heavy drops of rain.

As I have said, the texture, in nearly every phrase, is born from the subject, is the result of inspiration controlled by experience. Take, for example, these lines :

" I can stoop to pick up apples as they boom upon
    the ground,
  Choosing out the ripest as a gift to give them,
  And bribing them with fruit they'll turn to
    singing birds."

In this passage, as in Marvell's line :

    " Ripe apples drop about my head,"

the several " p's " give an impression of dewy bright roundness like that of the apples it is describing. In Mr. Sitwell's lines, we have, too, the feeling of ripeness and dewy warmth, given by the echoing warm " oo " and " U " sounds, whilst the smoothness and brightness of the skin, the change from warm sun to warm shadows as the branch moves, these are conveyed by the change from the long I sound to the dimmer I's.

Now let us consider the substance of these lines, describing Gargantua :

"Like smoke, proudly frozen smoke, these tufts
        of feathers
Framing his solar face of manly red,
His hair, thick as bear's fur, cropped for a shade,
With forehead of a bridge-pier's strength and bulk
Made formidable his emptiness."

In the first line the echoing O's (one being a dissonance), broadening the line and making it deep in colour, are perfectly fitted to reproduce for us the colour and bulk of Gargantua's face. In the third line :

"His hair, thick as bear's fur, cropped for a
        shade "

the three R's, each ending a word, cast a slight menacing shadow, since each of the words in question are words, not of one syllable, but of one syllable and a fraction each. The " d's " ending " cropped " and occurring in " shade " also cast a slight shadow, though less than that of the words ending with R.

It will not now be out of place to examine Mr. Sitwell's vowel technique in the lovely Serenade from the " Hundred and One Harlequins " :

" Sigh soft, sigh softly,
    rain-thrilled leaves,
    let not your careless hands
    stem the gold wind !
    Let not your greensleeves

K

swim in its breath,
as water flowing;
lest your thin hands
make gurgle down the crystal hills
the gaudy sun's pavilions
whence he distils those showered scents
whose virtue all true turtles croon
beneath their swaying palaces.
Sing low, then, turtles,
  Sigh soft, swift wind,
  and, fountains, cease your flutings.
  Melulla, now,
  lean on your balcony ! look down !
  My strings shall sing."

The melody of this is built on a very loose scheme
of E's, the only poignant vowels in the whole
poem (if we except the long I in " sigh " and the
long AI of " rain "), and a loose scheme of soft
warm dimmed I's.   These long E's give us a
long breath of air, a vista seen through the branches.
Otherwise, all is like the soft density and warmth
of the thickly-growing leaves ; this feeling being
given by the rarity of poignant vowels, and by the
fact, too, that Mr. Sitwell places his soft warm
" oo " and " u " sounds rather close together,
as in :

  " Whose virtue all true turtles croon,"

and

  " And, fountains, cease your flutings.
  Melulla, now."

("Now," of course, echoes the sound of "fountains.")

These "U" and "Oo" sounds are the most subtle of dissonances, so incredibly faint that they are almost assonances, sometimes sunny, sometimes dim, or dark, or dewy. The U in "virtue" is sharper and crisper than that in "true," whilst the sound of "true" is a minute fraction higher and cooler than that of "croon," and "flutings" sounds like a gush of water. The U in "Melulla" is nearly as deep and warm as that of "croon," and a lovely movement, a slow balance, is given to the word by the presence of the liquid L's. There is, indeed, a lovely internal pattern of these L's throughout the poem, giving a faint slow air, a sensation of rain falling from the leaves.

Throughout the poem, the faintest flutter, so faint that it is almost imperceptible, is caused by the pattern of internal R's sounding too like a sudden shower of raindrops falling (more quickly than those produced for us by the L's) from the heavy leaves. The D's ending two words placed close together—"Gold wind"—make the line slightly slower and longer.

Much of Mr. Sitwell's poetry is arranged on a melodic scheme of varying long and short I sounds, as in these lines from "New Water Music." (The Thirteenth Cæsar.)

"Cold night, cold night, made chiller by the water-
    glitter

Though the two who feast here have the sun's
    fire in their veins,
In fierce rivers burning,
And every time they move across the moonlight
They shimmer while they lift their arms, like
    opal, or lit water ;
The heaped apples they are eating
Like pebbles on a lake's bed glistening there,
Through many mirrors shown—
He speaks—
' My nightingale,
See how these leaves do hide us !
Their bunched and quilted thickness, since they're
    clouds, not trees,
Give closer cover than a leaf's thin blade,
But, like boughs, the wind can lift them,
And show us in the flooding light fixed and still,
The tents we lie in, all our nets for love,
On the wind's lips hanging, like the slaves who
    watch your eyelids ;
For ashore we have the clouds like leaves above us,
And at sea our sails against the wind's voice
    hoisted :
We can stay out in the full light, with not a
    bough to shelter us,

Or lie out in the cold main, a clump of stars,

With all our torches burning.'

She did not answer him but looked towards the
sea

Choosing among his words, which place she liked
best,

The apple in her hand, with its cool rind,
persuading her—

For it lay there shimmering in the moonbeams,

sharp and chill."

This varying pattern of long high I's and
soft warm dimmed I's produces, actually, the
feeling of the cool night, the long water-stretches,
the soft leaves ; produces, too, the actual movement
of the boat, the movement of the oars.

Again, it may not be out of place to enquire
which adds most to our experience—this fragment,
from Mr. Sitwell's poem, or the following poem,
also about the water. Again I will not mention
the name of the author, contenting myself with
remarking that the public is being taught to admire
his work, and that this poem is included in Mr.
Pound's " Active Anthology."

SLUGGISHLY

" Or with a rush
The river flows—

And none
is unaffected—

Think :
the clear stream

boiling at
the boat's wake

or—
a stench
your choice is—

And respond ?

crapulous
—having eaten

fouling
the water grass."

Now, one difference between the couplet and
the quatrain is that the couplet moves slower,
because of the gap, or slight hiatus, between two
lines and the next two lines. This is longer than
that which divides quatrains. But here we have
a poem in which the first syllables in most (though
not all) of the lines are unaccented and therefore
run with a rush, because the lines are so narrow
(there are only four, or two, or three, or one, and
in one case five syllables to each line). This rush,
therefore, casts a much heavier weight on the one
accented syllable of the line than would otherwise
be the case, and this causes a violent hiatus between
each line and the next. There is only one line
where this is not so ; the line :

" is unaffected "

has not quite such a violent hiatus between itself
and the next.

For what reason, then, was this poem put into
couplets, varied by an occasional triplet and an
occasional single line ?   It would not have mattered
if it were blocked, or in single lines throughout ;
it would not have mattered how it appeared.
But then, in my opinion, it would not have
mattered if it had not appeared at all.

Now let us take another poem by Mr. Sitwell
and compare it with a poem by a much admired
" new poet."

Here is Mr. Sitwell's poem :

The Fisherman.

" ' Do the fish still glitter in the water-pool ? '
    ' No, sir, they are netted and lie ready for your
        feasting.
They glittered in the water as a star would shine
If it steered into our vision
And through the day, as in the night,
Swam there to follow :
In point of light more brilliant than the race
        of stars
Shining in one body where it masks the sun,
The fish in this waterpool glitter like that star
        in air :
It turns like the star would do and lies there to
        look at you,
High against this glass wall that lies between,
With staring eyes dreaming,
Then will stretch and spread its fins,
And in a flash be gone,

Where shadow of the trees, or false sun, mars the
    water,
Safe hidden in this shade or flame.
Here, then, with limp nets we come to look for it,
And the meshes strain and open wide, once in
    the water,
Till the fish tap at those windows and now float
    inside.'
' Were they lively when you caught them ? '
' They leaped and sprang like horses till we held
    them fast.
We haul at the nets now and pull them out of
    water
And the fish come out with them like strong
    springs of silver,
They frisk and leap to get their breath like young
    horses
Galloping through the fields at early morning,
When the sun is strong already,
And the sun whips, like green rye, the running
    grassland.
Hold the net tightly as it comes to land,
Sagging, while water lines the strings and drops in
    runlets,
Safe upon the grass now while the fish still leap !
Close bound within the meshes so they cannot
    move,
Their lightning fettered, they are lifted shoulder-
    high
To drown there, stifling in the stiff, cold air.' "

The glittering fish, the glittering water, these
are brought before our eyes by the pattern of

sharp T's throughout the poem, and the depth
of the water is suggested by the falling dissonance
of the word " water " after " glitter," and of
" flash " coming in the line below " stretch " ;
and over and over again the lovely reflections in
the water are brought to us by the echoing vowel-
sounds :

" ' Were they lively when you ca[1]ught them ? '

   ' They le[3]aped and sprang like ho[1]rses till we held
       them fast.

   We ha[1]ul at the ne[4]ts now and pull them out of
       wa[1]ter

   And the fi[2]sh come out with them like strong
       spri[2]ngs of si[2]lver

   They fri[2]sk and le[3]ap to get their brea[3]th like young
       horses

   Galloping through the fie[3]lds at early morning.' "

The I sounds of " fish," " springs," " silver "
and " frisk " vary so faintly that the variations are
almost imperceptible, in depth and lightness, so
that not only have we the reflections in the water,
but also the light glittering, or a faint shadow
falling on the silver fish. The long high E
sounds lengthen and heighten the part of the line
in which they occur, till, partly by the power of
association, partly because of the actual sound,
the movement is that of the bright fish leaping
out of the water.

Where are the poeticisms in this poem ? Is it
not an experienced and transmuted record of an
actual everyday happening ? Have we not here
the common things of life made radiant by inspiration. In what way is it separated from the life
we have experienced, excepting by its greater
awareness ? And which most increases our consciousness, which most heightens our awareness,
our experience, this poem or the following prose
poem (also presumably about the water and fish),
by a writer named Theo Rutra—a poem which
has been much admired in certain American circles
because of the author's power of bringing new life
into the language, of creating new expressions.

" The loorabalboli glides through the algroves
suddenly turning upon itself. There is a spiral
spatter of silver. A thunderbolt lies in white.
The rolls drum down the hidden malvines, where
the gullinghales flap finwings casually. The pattern
of the salibri glint in the marlite. Then the
loorabalboli sings ' O puppets of the eremites, the
weed-maids fever love.' Send Octobus to shores
of clay ; thieve younglings out of sheaves of ice.
And troutrouts dance. There is a blish. A won-
derlope whirrs through the floom."

It has been held that Mr. Sitwell lives in a world
of unreality. Let us, therefore, take the following
lines from this poem :

VARIATION ON A THEME BY MARLOWE.

" *But how now stands the wind ?*
Into what corner peers my halcyon's bill ? "

Where is my halcyon ?   Is it hid in leaves ?
Does it run in the corn between those yellow
     sheaves ?
Does light like heavy myrrh cloy its wings
Flying from the sun's light while it sings ?

          .   .   .   .   .

But now, my halcyon, I call you back,
Come from the bough there that your weight
     sags down,
And float to my feet so that I smooth your
     plumes !
Tell me where does air lie softest,
In the West round the sun, or do the stars ride
     calm,
Their lamps burning level, never shaken in the
     tide ?
He peered in every corner and he chose the West,
And running to my feet he shook his wings and
     glittered,
Waiting for the ransom that he knew I held
     for him.
Stretch forth your bill, my halcyon, for this
     apple !
He took it from my hand, he spread his wings
     and flew with it,
And now I see him pecking it, safe-hid by boughs."

Let us consider for a moment the lovely floating
movement of the whole poem ; then the softness,
depth and warmth, like that of the halcyon's
feathers, and the slowing down of the line, as the
halcyon floats down from his dark bough, an impression which is produced by the two F's, the long

vowel-sounds, the deepening from the sound of
" float " to that of " smooth," and the faintly
deeper assonance of " plumes " in the line :

" And float to my feet so that I smooth your
    plumes."

After this we have echoes floating through the
leaves, in

    " Tell me where does air lie softest."

Compare this deep softness to this sudden change
of texture, wherein the lines brighten till they
become smooth and shining, glistening and bright-
coloured as the skin of the apple.

" And running to my feet he shook his wings and
    glittered,
    Waiting for the ransom that he knew I held
      for him.
    Stretch forth your bill, my halcyon, for this
      apple,"

softening again at the end of the last line, with its
soft A's, that are subtle changing echoes of
" ransom."

Mr. Sitwell's feeling of texture seems never to
fail him, and it is always born of his subject, and
is absolutely controlled, conveying the visual sense,
the oral sense, that he possesses in such a remarkable
degree. Here is a poem which conveys a sense of
the roundness of the fruit, of its coolness and of its
dark glossy leaves, by means of texture as well as
by means of imagery.

THE RED GOLD RAIN.

ORANGE TREE BY DAY.

" Sun and rain at work together
    Ripened this for summer weather ;
    Sun gave it colour tawny red
    And rain its life as though it bled ;
    In the long days full of fire
    Its fruit will cool us when we tire.
    Against the house-wall does it grow,
    With smooth stem like a fountain's flow,
    Dark are its leaves, a colder shade
    Than ever rock or mountain made ;
    When the wind plays soft they sing,
    For here the birds' songs never ring,
    Quite still the fruit that in a golden shower
    Will fall one day to flood this tower."

A sharpness is given to this lovely poem by the
long A sounds which echo through it, and the
changing shadows of the leaves are conveyed by
the way in which the accents shift from the first
to the second syllable of the lines. How lovely,
too, are the warm dark shadows, alternating with
the warm dream-like summer light, a change which
is conveyed by the dissonances, some accented,
others not, in the last two lines :

" Quite still the fruit that in a golden shower

Will fall one day to flood this tower."

Throughout the poem there is an internal pattern
of warm, dark, dewy " ou," " oo " and " u "
sounds, wavering subtly from depth to depth, and

sometimes growing upwards into a cooler O.
And at moments Mr. Sitwell gives the appearance
of lengthening a line by the means of using several
long vowels near together in a line which comes
directly after a line containing only one long vowel.

" The Italian Air " (" The Hundred and One
Harlequins ") is not by any means one of Mr.
Sitwell's best poems ; but the first quatrain and a
half have a singular perfection. After this, the poem
is, to my mind, less lovely, for in the last two lines of
the second quatrain, Mr. Sitwell suddenly changes
his scale, dwarfs it, and allows artificialities of an
unreal kind, the sort that were used by the minor
Elizabethans, to creep in (these two habits are
amongst his worst dangers), so that in the first
six lines we see him, if not entirely at his best,
nearly at his best, and then at his worst :

" In among the apple trees
   and on their echoing golden roofs,
   a singing shower rides on the breeze,
   and prints the grass with crystal hoofs.

The sighing music faints and fails
   among the far-off feathered boughs,
   the birds fold up their painted sails ;
   but voices sound, until they rouse

the sleeping birds and silent leaves."
                          etc.

Part of the beauty of the first six lines, the
feeling of pleasant happy summer weather and of
dew lying on warm bright leaves, is due to the
movement caused by the fact that the first accent
of the first line falls on the first, not second syllable,

and also to the fact that there is an additional
roundness, followed by length, due to the quiet
vowels and round " p " sound of " apple " followed
by the long E sound of " trees," a sound which is
given a faint shaking movement (growing forward)
by the presence of the R. Then we have the
varying echoing O sounds of the next two lines,
the echoes being sometimes higher, sometimes
lower, and varying slightly in length—with the
skilful use of an extra fraction of a syllable,
" shower," in the fourth line. Speaking of the
system of elision in the first volume of my " Pleasures
of Poetry " I said : " This device gives variation to
the line . . . the prosodist's pretended insensi-
tiveness as regards the elision of the letter W . . .
gives variation and an additional meaning, as in

" Of sorrow unfeigned and humiliation meet "—

a line which gives us the sound of sharp tears falling,
or of heavy rain or dew falling from some leafy
bough when disturbed by the footstep of a stranger
entering that enchanted sorrow."

In Mr. Sitwell's line, the sound of rain falling
from the leaves is far less heavy than that in Milton's
line, because in the latter " sorrow " has two heavy
vowels, and the vowel-sound with which the word
ends is followed immediately by another vowel
unpreceded by a consonant. The movement of
Mr. Sitwell's line is far quicker too—even if we leave
aside the fact that Milton's line is longer.

Mr. Sitwell's verse is full of exquisite and sharply
apprehended visual impressions, born into a texture,
a movement, that fits them perfectly, as in these

lovely and tender lines from " The Hermes of Praxiteles " (Canons of Giant Art).

" And rabbits, half as old as Bacchus, play in light ;
   Its tawny partisans they try to capture
   But at the very nibble edge these lift and rally,
   Slide from warm soft ear to rabbit bob-tail, just
      to puzzle
   And swing their tawny tassels to the powerless
      paws
   For rabbit hand to parry."

Note.—The phrase "tawny partisans" means the little specks of sunlight falling through the leaves and moving with them in the wind.

These sensual impressions, so accurate, so acute, add to our experience. Although Mr. Sitwell's green world of happy growing things is unruffled by any violence, so that the charge of inhumanity is brought against him by persons who dislike any poetry excepting that which is based only upon emotion, he yet gives us the world that we see, but do not know that we see—he increases our sense values.

Keats, in one of his letters (Vol. I, p. 245), wrote: " As to the poetical Character itself (I mean that sort of which, if I am anything, I am a Member ; that sort distinguished from the Wordsworthian or egotistical sublime ; which is a thing *per se* and stands alone) it is not itself—it has no self—it is every thing and nothing. It has no character— it enjoys light and shade ; it lives in gusts, be it foul or fair, high or low, rich or poor, mean or elevated. . . . A poet is the most unpoetical of anything in existence ; because he has no Identity—

he is continually in and filling some other Body.
The Sun, the Moon, the Sea and Men and Women
who are creatures of impulse are poetical and have
about them an unchangeable attribute—the poet
has none ; no identity—he is certainly the most
unpoetical of all God's Creatures. . . . It is a
wretched thing to confess ; but it is a very fact that
not one word I ever utter can be taken for granted
as an opinion growing out of my identical nature—
how can it, when I have no nature ? . . ."

This is true of nearly every great poet. If it
was true of Keats, it is also true of Mr. Sitwell,
and this is the reason both for his greatness and
his faults.

CHAPTER VII

EZRA POUND

In the year 1908, amidst the silvery tintinnabula-
tions of tea-spoons left over from the tea-parties of
the Victorian Aunts of Poetry, amidst the noise of
the shufflings of football boots, amidst the odd and
circumscribed movements (penned between wooden
wickets) of literary cricketers making their runs,
appeared a new poet who, heedless of wickets and
careless of tea-parties, walked with natural, free,
and beautiful movements according to the law of
his nature.

Tea-spoons were clashed, football boots were
hurled at the offender, in vain. Mr. Pound con-
tinued on his way, " disturbing "—to paraphrase a
later criticism of one of the tea-spoon school—
" the most mobile placidity."

This " disturbance " was, and still is, regarded
as an outrage, and after seventeen years of Mr.
Pound's example, we could still find a critic (in 1925)
praising that undisturbing placidity in the work of
one of the most admired Georgians, in these terms :
" The poet's . . . work has lost none of its
sweetness and artistry ; it is, as always, quietly
ascetic and lucid. Mr. S —— *never startles* (the
italics are mine). He plays a game that children
play, tracing a shadow on the wall :

' Until at last the lamp is brought,
The game is done, and now I see
The tangled scribble I have wrought
Grimacing at me mockingly.' "

But the revelation is, after all, an expected one, and not such as to disturb the most mobile placidity. A peculiar quality of certain types of the English countryside is made manifest in Mr. S——'s descriptive verse :

" But never a footstep comes to trouble
The rooks among the new-sown corn,
Or pigeons rising from the stubble,
And flashing brighter as they roam."

The revelations made by Mr. Pound, however, were not of an expected order, and placidity was much disturbed. I confess I am unable to understand why Mr. Pound's poems aroused so much fury, for, as Mr. Eliot has pointed out in his preface to Mr. Pound's Selected Poems, his " originality is genuine in that his versification is a *logical* development of the verse of his English predecessors," and " The earliest of the poems in this volume show that the first strong influences upon Pound, at the moment when his verse was taking direction, were those of Browning and Yeats. In the background are the 'nineties in general, and behind the 'nineties, of course, Swinburne and William Morris."
The intense vitality which inhabited every poem of Mr. Pound's, the sharp and clear visual sense, the apparent easiness of the movement—these

qualities, however, frightened readers with debilitated senses and no power of living. They were
alarmed at the fact that life was forming itself
into new rhythmic lines, which are yet a logical
development of those to which they were
accustomed.

They knew that (to quote Mr. Eliot once more)
"a man who devises new rhythms is a man who
extends and refines our sensibility ; and that is not
merely a question of technique " ; and of this
extension of sensibility they were afraid.

Of this fear, Mr. Pound paid no heed. He
developed his technique according to the necessities
of his time, and of his nature. In the Augustan
age, the outward structure of poetry was the result
of logic alone, whilst variations of speed, the feeling
of heat or of cold, the variations of different depths
and heights were produced by means of texture,
and was the result of sensibility and of instinct.
Poetry was therefore, in that age, as far as outward
structure was concerned, the sister of architecture ;
with the romantics, and their heightened vowel-
sense, resulting in different melodic lines, she
became the sister of music ; now she appears like
the sister of horticulture, each poem growing
according to the laws of its own nature, but in a
line which is more often the irregular though
entirely natural shape of a tree or of a flowering
plant—bearing leaves, bearing flowers, bearing fruit—
than a sharp melodic line, springing like a fountain.

In the work of a great artist like Mr. Pound,
however, the shape of the line, its outline and
colour are perfectly and miraculously balanced,

and may be claimed as being that "compound of freedom and of order" which, according to Mr. Pound's essay on Dolmetsch, constitutes a work of art. "It is perfectly obvious that art hangs between chaos on the one hand and mechanics on the other ; a pedantic insistence upon detail tends to drive out major form. A firm hold on major form makes for a freedom of detail."

In Mr. Pound's verse, the major form is in nearly every case visible—appearing sometimes as a clear pure melodic line, as in the earlier verse—sometimes as a stem from which flowers and leaves spring in abundance. I must, however, confess that greatly as I admire the major part of the Cantos, some of them do seem to me to resemble the lost luggage office at a railway station, with the trunks strewn about but carefully labelled. Mr. Pound has not, to the same degree, Mr. Eliot's supreme power of fusion ; for in many of the Cantos, although time that has been dead five hundred years ago lives again for us, it cannot be said that the events have the same simultaniety ; or, perhaps it would be more accurate to say that many of the events seem to have only a local or a temporary importance, and to be unconnected, excepting rhythmically, with the line. In fact, in them "a pedantic insistence upon detail tends to drive out major form." This complaint, however, only applies to a few of the Cantos.

It is easy enough to see why the general public— but not the public practised in reading poetry— might have failed to understand the Cantos if they had appeared before "Personæ" and "Ripostes,"

but it is impossible to guess why these should have
been found difficult. The poems in " Personæ "
and " Ripostes " are exquisitely balanced, and have
the pure melodic line which is only to be found in
the greatest lyric poetry, sometimes pausing and
sinking—as a fountain pauses and sinks before
springing afresh—sometimes growing like a flower.
This growth, which seems so inevitable, is in reality
the result of a miraculous art. How beautiful and
how significant, for instance, are the varying pauses—
like those of one who is about to " come again "
(be reincarnated) in this fragment from " Na
Audiart." The song seems some lonely air, strange
with age, heavy with dew, drifting through the gaps
in a ruined castle wall :

" Yea though thou wish me ill,
                    Audiart, Audiart,
Thy loveliness is here writ till,
                    Audiart,
Oh, till thou come again.
And being bent and wrinkled, in a form
That hath no perfect limning, when the warm
Youth dew is cold
Upon thy hands, and thy old soul
Scorning a new, wry'd casement,
Churlish at seemed misplacement,
Finds the earth as bitter
As now seems it sweet,
Being so young and fair
As then only in dreams,
Being then young and wry'd,
Broken of ancient pride,

Thou shalt then soften,
Knowing, I know not how,
Thou wert once she
                    Audiart, Audiart,
For whose fairness one forgave
                    Audiart,
Audiart
          Que be'm vols mal."

If we contrast this with the poignant sharpness
of the first verse of " The Spring " in " Lustra,"
we shall have some idea of Mr. Pound's subtlety
of hearing and of touch in these earlier poems.

" Cydonian Spring with her attendant train,
    Maelids and water-girls,
    Stepping beneath a boisterous wind from Thrace
    Throughout this sylvan place
    Spreads the bright tips,
    And every vine-stock is
    Clad in new brilliancies.
                        And wild desire
    Falls like black lightning.
    O bewildered heart,
    Though every branch have back what last year
        lost,
    She, who moved here amid the cyclamen,
    Moves only now a clinging tenuous ghost."

The sharpness of the first verse in this beautiful
poem—a sharpness which is like that of the " bright
tips " on the vine-branches—is caused partly by
the bright sound of " train," with its assonances
" Thrace " and " place " (" sylvan place " being

naturally softer, because of the soft S and C sounds),
partly by the strangeness of the assonances " tips,"
" is," " brilliancies," and by the clearness of the
sound of " water-girls." The S's in " Stepping,"
" boisterous," and the C in " Thrace " in the third
line, slow it down very faintly, as the boisterous
wind plays with the draperies of the attendant
train, and the sound of " throughout " in the next
line, echoes the sound of the wind.

In the lines :

> " And wild desire
> Falls like black lightning.
> O bewildered heart,"

the movement is much slower, mainly because
whereas in the first three lines the word " train,"
in the first, was echoed by the assonance " Thrace "
in the third line, and by its rhyme " place " in the
next—this giving it movement and swiftness—in
these later three lines there is neither assonance
nor rhyme, only the long double-edged sound of
" desire "—a word that has long echoes after its
two syllables and a half are over—the higher sound
of the first I in " lightning " (falling again to
earth in the second syllable) and the rather dead
sound of " O bewildered heart." After these three
lines, however, we have a wandering movement :

> " Though every branch have back what last year
>   lost,
> She, who moved here amid the cyclamen,
> Moves only now a clinging tenuous ghost."

The wandering slowness of the movement of this

is due partly to the " ch " in " branch " with the two S's in " last " and " lost," and partly to the fact that " lost " is a dark sinking echo of " last," and that the word which ends the last line " ghost " is a dissonance of " lost," which ends the next line but one above it. " Ghost," however, has a longer echo than " lost."

In such poems as these we find much to delight the ear and the visual sense ; but it is a little difficult to know why the " mobile placidity " of the public was disturbed, unless it were by the fact that Mr. Pound lives, obviously, in eternity and not in time as we know it. Audiart, Eleanor of the Cantos, the various Italian tyrants who inhabit these, are as living as Steffan who jostles them in their new life. This fact of giving life to the dead, especially in the later works, might perhaps disconcert those who do not believe in reincarnation upon this earth, but in the earlier works the reincarnation appeared easier. The reason for the fear felt in the presence of Mr. Pound's earlier poems may, perhaps, be found in the fact that " In the nineteenth century "—as William Morris pointed out in " News from Nowhere "—" there was a theory that art and imaginative literature ought to deal with contemporary life ; but they never did so ; for, if there was any pretence of it, the author always took care . . . to disguise or exaggerate, or idealize—in some way to make it strange ; so that, for all the verisimilitude there was, he might just as well have dealt with the time of the Pharaohs."

To Mr. Pound, however, persons who had been dead for a thousand years appeared as his

contemporaries, whilst the accidental accompaniments
of our present life—motor-cars, say—are as important
as, but no more important than, those of a thousand
years ago.   This, I imagine, is responsible for some
of the embarrassment felt before Mr. Pound's
earlier poems.   In addition to this, there was the
fact of his extraordinary learning—the fact that to
the unlearned, influences could be felt in his work,
but could not be traced to their source.   There
was, for instance, the influence of what Mr. Eliot
calls " the exact and difficult Provençal versification."   But there were, as well, easily recognizable
influences, such as that of Mr. Yeats' technique, of
William Morris, and of Browning.   But Mr. Pound's
rhythms are not roughly muscular like those of
Browning ; they are subtle and sensitive to an
almost unparalleled degree, and the muscular system
of these is the result of sensibility and is highly
trained, whereas Browning's was not.

In the midst of many technical influences—
which were, in the end, to form one of the most
highly-individual techniques of our time—Mr.
Pound's way of seeing was always his own.   Now,
one of the reasons why the pioneers in the arts are
so much disliked is that the public has got into the
way of thinking that man has always seen as he
sees now.   This is wrong.   Not only has he seen
with different eyes, but it is impossible that we
should all see alike at the present time, although the
crowd would prefer uniformity of sight.   The
modernist artist gives us the great chance of exerting
an individuality in seeing.   The older beauty, the
beauty of the Old Masters, is in the beauty of

species and of mass; the new beauty is highly
individualized and separate. The modern artist
is not concerned with things in the mass, he is
passionately interested in the fulfilling of the
destinies of the single individuals that make up the
mass—whether those individuals are men, or leaves,
or waves of the sea. The great quality of the Old
Masters in all the arts is force, used in the scientific
sense of the term—the binding together of the
molecules of the world. That is partly what makes
their sense of design so tremendous. The great
quality of the modern masters is an explosive
energy—the separating up of the molecules—
exploring the possibilities of the atom. This is at
once the quality and the danger of pioneer poetry.
One technical aim of the more accomplished of
the modernist poets is to reconcile this necessity
of exploring the possibilities of the atom with
the necessity for logical design and form.

In this aim Mr. Pound has been peculiarly
successful, attaining to the highest degree of expressiveness and uniting a rare power of compression
with an extraordinary flexibility.

The other great technical problem of the poetry
of today is that of the proper use of speech-rhythms,
but speech-rhythms made dynamic, not lowered in
vitality or slipping down hill. Mr. Pound in his
" How to Read " has said that " Great literature
is simply language charged with meaning to the
utmost possible degree." In producing this, Mr.
Pound shows what Mr. Eliot has claimed to be his
" complete and isolated superiority as a master of
verse-form." Mr. Pound has written of this matter

of dynamic language in " A.B.C. of Reading "
(Routledge), a work of much importance :

> " The changing of language is done in three
> principal ways : You receive the language as
> your race has left it, the words have meanings
> that have ' grown into the race's skin ' ; the
> Germans say ' wie in den Schnabel gewachsen,'
> as it grows in his beak. And the good writer
> chooses his words for their ' meaning,' but that
> meaning is not a set cut-off thing like the move
> of knight or pawn on a chess-board. It comes
> up with roots, with associations, with how and
> where the word is familiarly used, or where it
> has been used brilliantly or memorably. . . .
>
> You have to go almost exclusively to
> Dante's criticism to find a set of *objective*
> categories for words. Dante called words
> ' buttered ' and ' shaggy ' because of the
> different Noises they make. Or ' pesca et
> hirsuto,' combed and hairy."

Mr. Pound's sensibility to these differences was
always singularly acute, and must have appeared
shocking and strange to those readers who were
accustomed to the debility and meaningless texture
of the poems which were most prevalent in the
first decade of the twentieth century. This intense
life pulsated through all the early poems, taking
many different forms, until, in " Mauberley " it
found perfection.

In " Hugh Selwyn Mauberley " (" Life and
Contacts ") we have fixed for all time what is, at
once, the complete record of the life of an

individual and " the document of an era," to quote
Mr. Eliot's preface. The series of poems form a
comprehensive whole, and each poem is, to a
certain extent, dependent psychologically and
rhythmically upon the others. By this I mean that
the extraordinary flexibility of the rhythms can
only be apprehended to the fullest extent if the
poems are regarded not as separate poems, but as
parts of a complete poem.

This record of an age was first broken into
fragments by the different degrees of the pressure
of heat and cold which lay, or surged, beneath the
surface of the lines; it was then welded into a
whole by the artist's supreme mastery over his
material. I use the word " welded " and not
" fused " deliberately. The " broken images " of
Mr. Eliot's " The Waste Land " were *fused* into a
whole, and therein lies one of the differences between
the two poems. But the difference does not lie in
this alone, nor in the fact that " Mauberley " is the
life-story of an individual person and at the same
time " the document of an era," whereas " The
Waste Land " is not the record of an individual,
it is the life of all mankind. The difference lies,
too, in the fact that whereas " Mauberley " is the
record of an age, " The Waste Land " is a world,
and not the record of a world; the seemingly
dispersed fragments bear within themselves " correspondences," as Swedenborg has expressed it, as the
symbols which nature shows, bear correspondences
one with another, as the six-rayed snowflake resembles
the six-rayed crystal. It is true that this world has
been shattered; but the genius of the poet has

fused the fragments into an indivisible whole
once again.

The power over the material of poetry, shown
by Mr. Pound, is nothing short of astounding.
All expression is welded into an image and not
removed into a symbol, or squandered in a metaphor,
since these, as a means of expression, are necessarily
looser and more leisurely. The whole poem is
expressed in a variety of tuneless and broken
rhythms, sometimes hesitating and dropping, sometimes hurrying aimlessly; and these convey the
life of a figure moving adversely in a world where
the natural rhythms of life have broken down.

" For three years, out of key with his time,
    He strove to resuscitate the dead art
    Of poetry; to maintain ' the sublime '
    In the old sense.   Wrong from the start—

        .   .   .   .   .

    His true Penelope was Flaubert,
    He fished by obstinate isles;
    Observed the elegance of Circe's hair
    Rather than the mottoes on sundials.

    Unaffected by ' the march of events, '
    He passed from men's memory in ' au trentièsme,
    De son eage '; the case presents
    No adjunct to the Muses' diadem."

In this first poem he has, therefore, summed up
by the use of images strongly welded together, all
the interests of this artist's life. These images,
with the exception of one—" He fished by obstinate

isles "—need no explanation. But it is interesting
to know that this, to me, rather difficult phrase
has been explained by some critic—I think, by
Dr. Leavis—as conveying " his inveterate eclec-
ticism, his interest in various periods and cultures :
Provençal, Italian, Chinese, and so on."

The phrase " The mottoes on sundials " is a
deliberately withered and small understatement of
the passage of time, of the passing of an age, of the
gathering of the shadows of a new era.

In the second and third poems of " Mauberley,"
we have a concentrated essence of the present age,
the age of machine-made mass-production (which,
though they are formed by the inevitable rhythms
of machines of durable steel, have, themselves, no
rhythm—have no durability), the age of the stunting
and standardizing of the spirit, the age which has
decreed that the giant cannot reach to heights
beyond the stretch of the dwarf, that the dwarf
cannot explore crevices and hiding-places that are
unknown to the giant.

This age is produced before our eyes by the most
miraculous control of technique, which allows
for all looseness, all heightening and slowing of
speed in the medium. Indeed, what appear,
at first, to be the ordinary and careless
rhythms of speech are, in reality, the result of an
extraordinary sensibility of technique ; the poet
produces, by the deliberate tunelessness, and by
the variation between lamed, guttering-down, or
over-hurried and feverish rhythms, this age which,
mass-produced by a too-mechanical rhythm, has,
in itself, no rhythm.

> " The age demanded an image
>   Of its accelerated grimace,
>   Something for the modern stage,
>   Not, at any rate, an Attic grace ;
>
>   Not, not certainly, the obscure reveries
>   Of the inward gaze ;
>   Better mendacities
>   Than the classics in paraphrase !
>
>   The ' age demanded ' chiefly a mould in plaster,
>   Made with no loss of time,
>   A prose kinema, not, not assuredly, alabaster
>   Or the ' sculpture of rhyme.' "

The crumbling sandstone-like sound of " age," finding its refuge in " image " (its echo), then crumbling down into the still softer echoes of their assonances in the next line : " accelerated . . . grimace . . ." (the softness is that of something which should be hard, but which has decayed into softness)—the significance of these sounds is deliberate. And the echo of these sounds is heard again in the next verse : " gaze," " paraphrase " ; and the sound is less persistent than that of " age " or of " image," more persistent that that of " grimace," " grace."

In the next poem, in the fifth verse, we have a muffling, thickening arrangement of F's, with one slightly longer V, and these sounds convey the thickening of human sensibilities :

> " Faun's flesh is not to us,
>   Nor the saint's vision.
>   We have the Press for wafer ;
>   Franchise for circumcision."

The fourth poem is an almost unbearably moving record of the war—an evocation of the men who arose from the dead, only to walk " eye-deep " once more, into the new hell that the old men had prepared for them.

" . . . Died some, pro patria,
                    non ' dulce ' non ' et decor ' . . .
walked eye-deep in hell
believing in old men's lies, then unbelieving
came home, home to a lie,
home to many deceits,
home to old lies and new infamy ;
usury age-old and age-thick
and liars in public places.

Daring as never before, wastage as never before.
Young blood and high blood,
fair cheeks, and fine bodies ;

fortitude as never before.

frankness as never before
disillusions as never told in the old days,
hysterias, trench confessions,
laughter out of dead bodies."

In this great poetry (I have only quoted part of the section from which it comes), the springs of the rhythm are broken ; the beginning of each line starts up as a broken automaton might start up, at the opening of each new day, to begin its mechanical gamut of meaningless and useless toil. Then the line struggles to its close—sometimes

M

moving stiffly and automatically as if the spring
still controlled it :

> (" Young blood and high blood,
>   fair cheeks, and fine bodies ; ")

Sometimes sinking into nothingness :

> (" Daring as never before, wastage as never
>   before ").

Sometimes stretching hopelessly outward.

In the sixth poem " Yeux Glauques," we have
gone back to the spiritual preparations for the
present time, and to the discordance (since this is
the history of an artist) between the particular
morality of Gladstone, Ruskin and " fœtid
Buchanan " and that of Swinburne, Rossetti and
Burne-Jones. It is, I think, one of the least
interesting poems in the sequence. In the next,
" Siena Mi Fe ; Disfecemi Maremma," we have
the age that resulted from this—the amalgamation
of the two moralities in the eighteen nineties
imaged in the death of Lionel Johnson, who . . .

> " . . . showed no trace of alcohol
>   At the autopsy, privately performed—
>   Tissue preserved—the pure mind
>   Arose toward Newman as the whisky warmed."

This crumbling, shrinking, into the dry sound
of the last verse,

> " M. Verog, out of step with the decade,
>   Detached from his contemporaries,
>   Neglected by the young,
>   Because of these reveries."

The rhythm of the ninth poem, " Mr. Nixon,"

has a miraculously sure poise and certainty, repro-
ducing, as it does, the different fat stretches of
self-assurance conveyed in Mr. Nixon's conversation
—stretches which fall now and then into a pause,
as Mr. Nixon reflects on his less certain past, when
he, too, was obliged to

> " Consider
> Carefully the reviewer."

The rhythm of this section differs greatly from
the timed hesitancies of No. XII, where the poet,
awaiting " the Lady Valentine's commands," realizes
the place of poetry in the Cosmos.

> " Poetry, her border of ideas,
>   The edge, uncertain, but a means of blending
>   With other strata
>   Where the lower and higher have ending ;
>
>   A hook to catch the Lady Jane's attention,
>   A modulation toward the theatre,
>   Also, in the case of revolution,
>   A possible friend and comforter."

Then, after the beautifully formed, but less
intrinsically interesting " Envoi " we come to the
section called " Mauberley," which is a quintessence
of the poems which precede it.   In the first section,
an extra emphasis is laid on

> " His true Penelope
> Was Flaubert,"

and from this emphasis we gather that the poet
passed his life in pursuing or returning to art for
the sake of art—Flaubert being the symbol of the
pure artist.

The lines :

> " And his tool
> The engravers.
>
> Firmness,
> Not the full smile,
> His art, but an art
> In profile ;
>
> Colourless
> Pier Francesca,"

concentrate, in one image, his devotion to the pure outline of art, and, in its reference to " art in profile " explains his attitude towards life.

The firmness and exquisiteness of the " profile " has changed, however, in the next poem, to weakness, to hesitation. This poem I have quoted whole, together with Dr. Leavis' comments on it, in the first chapter of this book. It is a poem whose verses cannot be separated from each other with any success, or the sense of " bewilderment " conveyed by the drifting movement, the interweaving of the thin strands of sound would be lost. The " Thirty-Three Cantos " present far greater difficulties than " Mauberley "—at least to a reader who, like myself, has not the advantage of a classical education.

In some cases we have the difficulty presented by the extreme intricacy of the interweaving of events, growing out of each other according to the laws of nature ; in others, we are presented with a still greater difficulty, that of events which are, actually, echoes of each other separated by gaps in time. These gaps in time have been abolished by

the poet, and echo and original have been welded into
what Mr. Yeats, writing of the Cantos in " A
Packet for Ezra Pound " has called " an Archetypal
Event "—present the appearance of simultaniety—
all time is welded into the present time.

We have, also, the problem of the presence of
Archetypal Persons—of the building up into one
body of various characteristics that have persisted,
throughout many ages, in many bodies ; as an
example of this simultaniety, we may point to the
fusion of the idea of the banking-house of Kahn
with the idea of Kubla Kahn. Sometimes, again,
we find splinters of these Archetypal Persons,
called by many different names, and these again
are splintered up into many still thinner wedges of
personalities expressing themselves by sound.

It will, no doubt, be possible in the course of
time to realize the design of this monumental work
as a whole ; at the present, this realization is
difficult. Mr. Yeats, in his " Packet for Ezra Pound "
has given us the most valuable help that could
be found, in his record of a conversation that he
had with Mr. Pound. . . . " He explains that
it will, when the hundredth Canto is finished,
display a structure like that of a Bach Fugue. There
will be no plot, no chronicle of events, no logic of
discourse, but two themes, the descent into Hades
from Homer, a Metamorphosis from Ovid, and
mixed with these medieval or modern historical
characters. He has tried to produce that picture
Porteous commended to Nicholas Poussin in ' Le
Chef d'oeuvre Inconnu ' where everything rounds
or thrusts itself without edges, without contours—

conventions of the intellect—from a splash of tints
and shades, to achieve a work as characteristic of
the art of our time as the paintings of Cezanne,
avowedly suggested by Porteous, as 'Ulysses' and
its dream association of words and images, a poem
in which there is nothing that can be taken out and
reasoned over, nothing that is not a part of the
poem itself. He has scribbled on the back of an
envelope certain sets of letters that represent
emotions or archetypal events—I cannot find any
other adequate definition—A B C D and then
J K L M, and then each set of letters repeated, and
then A B C D inverted and this repeated, and then
a new element of X Y Z, then certain letters that
never recur and then all sorts of combinations of
X Y Z and J K L M and A B C D and D C B A and
all set whirling together. He has shown me upon
the wall a photograph of a Cosimo Tura decoration
in three compartments, in the upper the Triumph of
Love and the Triumph of Chastity, in the middle
Zodiacal signs, and in the lower certain events in
Cosimo Tura's day. The descent and the metamorphosis—A B C D and J K L M—his fixed
elements, took the place of the Zodiac, the
archetypal persons—X Y Z—that of the Triumphs,
and certain modern events—his letters that do not
recur—that of those events in Cosimo Tura's day.

"I may, now that I have recovered leisure, find
that the mathematical structure, when taken up
into imagination, is more than mathematical, that
seemingly irrelevant details fit together into a single
theme, that here is no botch of tone and colour—
Hodos Chameleontos—except for some odd corner

where one discovers beautiful detail like that finely
modelled foot in Porteous' disastrous picture."

Here, then, we have the Cantos as seen through
the eyes of a great poet, and one who has been in
constant communion with Mr. Pound.

In the review of the Cantos which appeared in
Hound and Horn (Winter, 1931) and which has
been quoted by Dr. Leavis, we are told that "Mr.
Pound's documentation is a device, a technic.
History and literature are for him a mine of images,
and his purpose is to fix certain of these images in a
lasting, orderly design, without reference to a
philosophy or to any system of teleological
principles. Now whether the historical fact, the
Image, be the blowing of apricot-blossoms from
east to west, or a narcotic charge preferred against
Frank Robert Iriquois of Oklahoma City, or the
departure of Anchises from Troy, it is a detail of
supreme importance to the frieze, a note of supreme
importance to the *mélos*, which is the poem as a
whole. The poet, as I have observed, uses images
precisely as another poet would use metaphors or,
even more simply, chromatic words. These images
have no 'hidden meaning.' Malatesta, Frank
Robert Iriquois, the apricot-blossoms, are no more
'puzzling' than Shakespeare's 'encarnadine' in
the verse about the multitudinous seas. It is true
that if you have enough Latin to be able to associate
'encarnadine' with 'flesh,' 'carnation' and the
other rich warm 'carn' words, you will derive
more enjoyment from the verse than will X, who
knows only that 'encarnadine' is a euphemism for
'redden'; but you will 'understand' the verse

not a whit better than your less-informed friend. Therefore, the criticism that XXX Cantos is incomprehensible is a false criticism ; and I have gone into it at some length because it seems to be the objection that is being most strongly urged against the poem. The Cantos will baffle persons who are willing to be baffled, but this is so in the case of any considerable poem.

" The Cantos may be described as an epic of timelessness. That is to say, the poem represents Mr. Pound's endeavour to manage an arrest of time. Roughly the method is that of identification or fusion of image."

The reviewer in *Hound and Horn* does, I think, underrate the difficulties to be found in Mr. Pound's many allusions to rather obscure current events of no particular intrinsic interest. Mr. Pound cannot, however, be blamed because his profound scholarship leads the reader of no great classical education into other difficulties. But neither must the average reader be blamed for not knowing, for instance, that the first Canto is a paraphrase from the translation of Homer, accomplished in about the year 1530 by Andreas Divus. Mr. Pound means this, evidently, to form a bridge between the cultures of the two ages.

Those readers who are acquainted with Golding's translation of the eighth book of the Metamorphoses, or who have read Mr. Pound's " Pavannes and Divisions," will recognize the otherwise mysterious " Schoeney " in Canto II : Helen, the unnamed menace, is spoken of as having the voice of Schoeney's daughters :

" And poor old Homer blind, blind, as a bat,
Ear, ear for the sea-surge, murmur of old men's
    voices :
' Let her go back to the ships,
Back among Grecian faces, lest evil come on our own,
Evil and further evil, and a curse cursed on our
    children,
Moves, yes she moves like a goddess
And has the face of a god
        And the voice of Schoeney's daughters,
And doom goes with her in walking,
Let her go back to the ships,
        Back among Grecian voices.' "

Schoeney is Schoenus, the father of Atalanta, and
in Golding's translation of the eighth book of the
Metamorphoses, we find the lines :

" Atlant, a goodly Ladie one
    Of Schoeneyes daughters. . . ."

The passage that I have quoted from the " Thirty-
Three Cantos " is an especially beautiful and significant one. In the sound, in the echo of the second
one-syllabled word, " sea-surge," of " murmur of
old men's voices," we are given an evocation of the
fact that the sea-surge is immemorially old, has
an immemorable wisdom echoing through time.
The " sea-surge " and the " murmur of old men's
voices " are then separate entities, but they have
come together, and are one, or at least are scarcely
separate in the ear of age and wisdom. The whole
passage has the movement, the majestic sound of
waves breaking in all their different splendour :

" And doom goes with her in walking."

In that great line we have the whole sound, gathered throughout the ages, of the sea.

Part of the magic conveying the sound of the sea is obtained by the echoes which come from time to time ; the sound of " surge," for instance, is echoed, three lines further on, by the less-long sound of " curse," repeated twice, like the sound of a wave gathering itself and spreading outwards :

> " Evil and further evil, and a curse cursed on our children,"

and the sound of " moves " in the line :

> " Moves, yes she moves like a goddess,"

has the far deeper echo of " doom " after the interval of a line, a sound which contains all the hollowness and reverberation of the sea-depths. There is an echo, too, at the end of the lines :

> " And the voice of Schoeney's *daughters*
> And doom goes with her in *walking*."

The whole sound is that of the sea, with all the sea's depth.

The first two Cantos are a magnificent achievement. The wide stretch of the sea, the scarcely perceptible movement of the ripples, the clear sea-airs, are all conveyed by means of the fluctuating lengths of the opening lines of the first Canto, and by the shifting of the first accent from the first syllable to the second syllable of the line ; and by the fact also that the second line is only part of a phrase and is therefore part of a terrific sweeping movement, with a pause wherein the wind gathers :

"And then went down to the ship,
 Set keel to breakers, forth on the godly sea, and
 We set up mast and sail on that swart ship,
 Bore sheep aboard her, and our bodies also
 Heavy with weeping, and winds from sternward
 Bore us out onward with bellying canvas,
 Circe's this craft, the trim-coiffed goddess."

The Canto's first line finds us sailing over a sea (the Canto begins where my quotation begins), and if there is a more terrific sweeping-onward of movement (that is yet perfectly smooth) to be found in all English poetry, I have yet to find it.

A small wave comes in the middle of the sixth line, with the faint stresses, placed in immediate juxtaposition, of "out onward," breaks beneath the ship, and the ship sweeps on again.

Both these opening Cantos have the most strangely accurate, sharp, acutely observed visual impressions, like the portrait of the seal in the second Canto:

"Sleek head, daughter of Lir,
            eyes of Picasso,
 Under black fur-hood, lithe daughter of Ocean;
 And the wave run in the beach-groove."

The movement of the ship seems to grow faster, in the second Canto, with the shortening of the lines, and with the tight effect of the one-syllabled ending of some of the lines, followed by the strong accent on the first syllable of the next line, alternating with the loosening caused by certain female endings:

        "Ship stock-fast in sea-swirl,
 Ivy upon the oars, King Pentheus,

> Grapes with no seed but sea-foam,
> Ivy in scupper-hole."

Indeed, the whole of these two Cantos may be said to be a miracle of the transfusion of sense into sound ; or rather, of the fusion of the two.

In the first part of the second Canto, the first accent of the lines shifts its place perpetually, though the movement is not elaborately contrapuntal :

> " And where was gunwale, there now was vine-
> trunk,
> And tenthril where cordage had been,
> grape-leaves on the rowlocks,
> Heavy vine on the oarshafts,
> And, out of nothing, a breathing,
> hot breath on my ankles,
> Beasts like shadows in glass,
> a furred tail upon nothingness.
> Lynx-purr, and heathery smell of beasts,
> where tar smell had been,
> Sniff and pad-foot of beasts,
> eye-glitter out of black air.
> The sky overshot, dry, with no tempest,
> Sniff and pad-foot of beasts,
> fur brushing my knee-skin,
> Rustle of airy sheaths,
> dry forms in the *æther*.
> And the ship like a keel in ship-yard,
> slung like an ox in smith's sling,
> Ribs stuck fast in the ways,
> grape-cluster over pin-rack,
> void air taking pelt.

Lifeless air become sinewed,
        feline leisure of panthers,
Leopards sniffing the grape shoots by scupper-hole,
Crouched panthers by fore-hatch,
And the sea blue-deep about us,
        green-ruddy in shadows,
And Lyæus, ' From now, Acœtes, my altars,
Fearing no bondage,
        Fearing no cat of the wood,
Safe with my lynxes,
        feeding grapes to my leopards,
Olibanum is my incense,
        the vines grow in my homage.'
The back-swell now smooth in the rudder-chains,
Black snout of a porpoise
        where Lycabs had been,
Fish-scales on the oarsmen.
        And I worship.
I have seen what I have seen.
        When they brought the boy I said :
' He has a god in him,
        though I do not know which god.'
And they kicked me into the fore-stays.
I have seen what I have seen :
        Medon's face like the face of a dory,
Arms shrunk into fins. And you, Pentheus,
Had as well listen to Tiresias, and to Cadmus,
        or your luck will go out of you.
Fish-scales over groin-muscles,
        lynx-purr amid sea . . .
And of a later year,
        pale in the wine-red algæ,

If you will lean over the rock,
                the coral face under wave-tinge,
Rose-paleness under water-shift,
                Ileuthyeria, fair Dafne of sea-bords,
The swimmer's arms turned to branches,
Who will say in what year,
                fleeing what band of tritons,
The smooth brows, seen, and half seen,
                now ivory stillness."

The reason for the more-embodied and hard-outlined movement, for its condensation, may be found in the lines :

            " void air taking pelt.
Lifeless air become sinewed."

In this miraculous poetry Mr. Pound, by some enchantment, fuses the sense of the beasts with the sense of the oncoming tempest.

The rhythms have an extraordinary variety, a lovely flexibility and inevitability that is sometimes like " the feline leisure of panthers," or like the fluctuating, flowing, waving sound of the airs coming from some immortal sea. The echoes indeed, and the sounds that originate them, vary, as do the sounds and echoes in certain of Milton's songs, from sea-air to sea-air, from wave to wave, as the beauty of the line lengthens and then runs back again.

At the end of the second Canto we have an example of this consummate power of variation. For after the plunging forward of the ship, after the embodying of the beasts, beasts with fur as thick and dark as clouds, with movements like

sinewed lightning, in an air " without tempest,"
we have this sudden dew-laden peace that is not
the result of association alone, but also of the
lengthening of the line, the scarcely perceptible
beat of the accents, and of what is practically an
absence of Cæsura :

" And we have heard the fauns chiding Proteus
        in the smell of hay under the olive-trees,
    And the frogs singing against the fauns in the
        half-light,
    And. . . ."

Now let us take the strange and subtle rhythm
of the first two lines in the fourth Canto :

" Palace in smoky light,
    Troy but a heap of smouldering boundary stones,"

in which part of the strangeness and mournfulness
is brought about by the assonance-dissonance
scheme, and by the length of the dark vowel-sounds
in " smoky," " smouldering," " stones," changing
to the high breaking sound of " Troy," and its
high chilly dissonance, the first vowels in
" boundary," that sinks again into the long stretch
of sound in the word " stones."

Then, shortly afterwards, we have the strange
circling, windy sound of these lines :

" And by the curved, carved foot of the couch,
        claw-foot and lion head, an old man seated
    Speaking in the low drone . . . :
                        Ityn !
    Et ter flebiliter, Ityn, Ityn !

> And she went toward the window and cast her
>   down,
> All the while, the while, swallows crying :
>   Ityn !
> ' It is Cabestan's heart in the dish.'
> ' It is Cabestan's heart in the dish ?
> ' No other taste shall change this ! ' "

In this extremely beautiful and poignant fragment we are given by rhythm and by the use of
certain vowels, the cry of the swallows, and their
swift and circling movements, and the very strangeness of these sounds embodied in human speech
give us the strangeness and the poignancy of the
tragedy.

Mr. Pound lives with the men on the ships at
Scios and with Cabestan, whose heart was in the
dish, and with his lady . . . but the modern
financiers and grafters who appear in the Canto
seem like figures in a tapestry.   And the
tapestry is not, to this reader, of any superlative
interest.

Mr. Ronald Bottrall, in a very finely-reasoned
essay on the Cantos, in *Scrutiny*, explains that
" after the account of the Austrian commercial
representative living in America as an agent for
raw material and munitions of war, there follows
a commentary on the Carranza régime in Mexico
and the problem of mineral and mining rights.
Next comes an incident related by Lamont (Tommy
Baymont) to Steffens [this part of the Cantos
is founded on the Autobiography of Lincoln
Steffens] to indicate the limits of power of the

Morgan firm when confronted by the gangster activities of 'Diamond Jim Brady.' . . . Another passage seems to deal with a meeting of the Morgan partners, but the key is missing."

Now, the raw material of this passage does not, in itself, form interesting reading. The speech-rhythms are easy, but even this easiness does not convey any pleasure to this reader, at any rate. The lines are excellently constructed, but do not give that extreme shock, that awakening of the intelligence or the sensibility, or both, that is given by great poetry. Coleridge, in " Biographia Literaria " says that " There are . . . poems . . . replete with every excellence of thought, image, and passion, which we expect or desire in the poetry of the milder muse, and yet so worded that the reader sees no one reason either in the selection or the order of the words why he might not have said the very same in an appropriate conversation, and cannot conceive how indeed he could have expressed such thoughts otherwise, without loss or injury to their meaning."

This might, by modern critics, be taken as supreme praise ; but we must remember the inclusion of the word : " Yet. . . ."

In the passage to which I refer, the voice is not that of one speaking " above a mortal mouth." But in the superb fusion of inspiration, image, and ound of, say, the first two Cantos, of the IV Canto, and of the two appalling Cantos about the material hell of this modern world, the voice *does* speak above a mortal mouth.

The following lines, however, to my mind would

N

not be interesting in prose. They are no more
interesting in poetry :

" Governed.   Governed the place from a train,
  Or rather from three trains, on a railway,
  And he'd keep about three days ahead of the lobby,
  I mean he had his government on the trains,
  And the lobby had to get there on horseback ;
  And he said : ' Bigod its damn funny,
  Own half the oil in the world, and can't get enough
  To run a government engine ! '
  And then they jawed for two hours,
  And finally Steff said : ' Will you fellows show me
      a map ? '
  And they brought one, and Steff said :
  ' Waal what are those lines ? ' ' Yes, those straight
      lines ? '
  ' Those are roads.'   And ' what are those lines,
  The wiggly ones ? '   ' Rivers.'
  And Steff said : ' Government property ? '

  So two hours later an engine went off with the
      order :
  How to dig without confiscation.

  And Tommy Baymont said to Steff one day :
  ' You think we run it, lemme tell you,
  We bought a coal mine, I mean the mortgage
      fell in,
  And you'd a' thought we could run it.

  Well I had to go down there meself, and the
      manager
  Said " Run it ? of course we can run it,
  We can't sell the damn coal."

So I said to the X and B Central
—you'd say we boss the X and B Central ?—
I said : " You buy your damn coal from our
    mine."
And a year later they hadn't ; so I had up the
    directors,
And they said . . . well anyhow, they couldn't
    buy the damn coal.
And next week ole Jim came, the big fat one,
With the diamonds, and he said : " Mr. Baymont,
You just *must* charge two dollars more
A ton fer that coal. And the X and B will
Take it through us." ' "

The argument may be put forward that here we
have the record of the new state of the world ; the
defence may be put forward that here is a perfect
balance of the depredations of the Italian tyrants—
of the trade-voyages of the Venetians : that,
perhaps, Steffens is a modern counterpart of the
Doge. Or again, it may be said that the

" Ear, ear for the sea-surge, murmur of old men's
    voices "—

changing and withering to the

        " rattle of old men's voices.
And then the phantom Rome,
        marble narrow for seats "—

changing again, through the lolling sound of the
first two lines of the XII Canto :

        " And we sit here
            under the wall,"

to the dead rattling sound of

" Arena romana, Diocletian's, les gradins
          quarante-trois rangées en calcaire.
     Baldy Bacon
          bought all the little copper pennies in Cuba : "

finds another, and horrible disfiguring metamorphosis in the voice of Steffens and his confederates.
It may be said, too, that at last all vain human
ambition, sounding so hideously through the blustering voices of the modern emperors of industry, is
ennobled and transmuted into these great lines—
linked up, as they are, with the themes of the first
two Cantos :

          " ' Feared neither death nor pain for
               this beauty ;
     If harm, harm to ourselves. '
     And beneath : the clear bones, far down,
     Thousand on thousand.
          ' What gain with Odysseus,
               They that died in the whirlpool.
     And after many vain labours,
     Living by stolen meat, chained to the rowing
          bench,
     That he should have a great fame
          And lie by night with the goddess ?
     Their names are not written in bronze
          Northeir rowing-sticks set with Elpenor's ;
     Nor have they mound by sea-bord.
          That saw never the olives under Spartha
     With the leaves green and then not green,
          The click of light in their branches ;
     That saw not the bronze hall nor the ingle
     Nor lay there with the queen's waiting maids,

Nor had they Circe to couch-mate, Circe Titania,
Nor had they meats of Kalüpso
Or her silk skirts brushing their thighs.
Give ! What were they given ?
    Ear-wax.
Poison and ear-wax,
    And a salt grave by the bull-field,
neson amumona, their heads like seacrows in the
    foam,
Black splotches, sea-weed under lightning ;
Canned beef of Apollo, ten cans for a boat load ?
Ligur ' ' aoide.' "

These arguments may be put forward, and there is much to be said for them. But the fact of this balance in design does not convert the Steffens lines into the equal of the magnificent passage just quoted. The passage about Steffens and Baymont seems like an ordinary conversation taken down by a secretary on the typewriter. It is a flat record, and that is all.

If we compare those lines with any, taken at random, from the huge appalling smoky and Tartarean horror of Cantos XIV and XV, we shall see the difference between great poetry and an uninspired record :

" howling, as of a hen-yard in a printing-house,
    the clatter of presses,
the blowing of dry dust and stray paper,
fœtor, sweat, the stench of stale oranges,
dung, last cess-pool of the universe,
mysterium, acid of sulphur,
the pusillanimous, raging ;

plunging jewels in mud,
     and howling to find them unstained ;
sadic mothers driving their daughters to bed with
    decrepitude,
sows eating their litters,"

.   .   .   .   .

Or these deliberately shambling lines :
" The slough of unamiable liars,
     bog of stupidities,
malevolent stupidities, and stupidities,
the soil living pus, full of vermin,
dead maggots begetting live maggots, slum owners,
usurers squeezing crab-lice, panders to authority,
pets-de-loup, sitting on piles of stone books,
obscuring the texts with philology,
     hiding them under their persons,
the air without refuge of silence,
     the drift of lice, teething,
and above it the mouthing of orators,
     the arse-belching of preachers."
These passages, and such lines as

" Flies carrying news, harpies dripping shit through
    the air "

are great poetry, and a living evocation of the
modern hell, the final state of the world which is
cursed by

" the old man sweeping leaves "

" Damned to you, Midas, Midas lacking a Pan."

In these two lines, this great poet has indeed shown
us the state of our modern world—that shallow
covering for the hell of the XIV and XV Cantos.

CHAPTER VIII

NOTES ON INNOVATIONS IN PROSE

IN the hands of the minor craftsmen of the last twenty-five years of the nineteenth century and the first decade of this, language, as we have seen, had settled down into stagnant rhythmic patterns, and patterns to which our eyes, our minds, were so accustomed that we no longer noticed them ; they were unliving and insignificant. Language had become, not so much an abused medium, as a dead and outworn thing, in which there was no living muscular system. Then came the rebirth of the medium, and this was effected, as far as actual vocabularies were concerned, very largely by such prose writers as Mr. James Joyce and Miss Gertrude Stein. Prose writers, naturally, scarcely come into the scope of my book ; but as the anarchic breaking up and rebuilding of sleepy families of words and phrases, for which Miss Stein is responsible, the creation of a new vocabulary, for which Mr. Joyce is responsible, must, in the future, affect poetry very greatly, it will not be amiss to examine them. The most interesting account of this revolution, as far as I know, is contained in an essay by Mr. Eugene Jolas " The Revolution of Language and James Joyce " (*Transition*, February, 1928). This essay, indeed, is of acute interest and importance.

Mr. Jolas reminds us that in the past " It was usually the people who, impelled by their economic or political lives, created the new vocabularies. The vates, or poetic seer, frequently minted current expressions into a linguistic whole."

Now, in the gigantic upheaval of the present age, a few changed, sharpened, or new expressions will not meet our needs. As Mr. Jolas says : " The disintegration of words and their subsequent reconstruction on other planes constitute some of the most important phenomena of our age."

Mr. Jolas has explained these disintegrations and reconstructions, these experiments, the reasons underlying them and the results obtained by them, more clearly than I can hope to do ; and as innovations in prose do not come within the scope of my book, though, because of their enormous intrinsic importance, and because of the influence they will exert over poetry in the future, they cannot be passed over in silence, I will confine myself to quoting some of Mr. Jolas' comments on Mr. Joyce and Miss Stein, and to quoting various passages from the works of these writers in order that the reader may gain some idea of their quality.

Mr. Jolas says of Mr. Joyce : " In Ulysses and in his still unnamed novel (he) was occupied in exploding the antique logic of words. . . . In his supertemporal and multispatial composition, language is born anew before our eyes. Each chapter has an internal rhythm differentiated in proportion to the contents. The words are compressed into stark blasting accents. They have the tempo of immense rivers flowing to the sea. Nothing that the world of appearance shows seems to interest him " [*Note.*—There I do not agree, E. S.] " except in relation to the huge philosophic and linguistic pattern he has undertaken to create. A modern mythology is being evolved against the curtain of the past, and a plane of infinity emerges. The human being across his words becomes the passive agent of some strange and inescapable destiny."

Of Miss Stein, he says that " In structurally spontaneous composition in which words are grouped rhythmically she succeeds in giving us her mathematics of the word, clear, primitive, and beautiful."

To see Mr. Joyce's style at its most beautiful, to share with him his recreation of our old and outworn visual world through the word, we cannot do better than to quote this intensely lovely and strange passage from " Three Fragments from Work in Progress " (Paris, Black Sun Press).

" Nuvoletta in her lightdress, spunn of sixteen shimmers was looking down on them, leaning over the bannistars and listening all she childishly could. She was alone. All her nubied companions were asleeping with the squirrels. . . . She tried all the winsome wonsome ways her four winds had taught her. She tossed her sfumastelliacinous hair like la Princesse de la Petite Bretagne, and she rounded her mignons arms like Mrs. Cornwallis West and she smiled over herself like the beauty of the image of the post of the daughter of the queen of the Emperour of Irelande and she sighed after herself as were born to bride with Tristran Tristior Tristissimus. . . .

" O, how it was dusk ! From Vallée Maraia to grasyaplaina, dorminant Echo ! Ah dew ! ah dew ! It was so dusk that the tears of night began to fall, first by ones and twos, then by threes and fours, at last by fives and sixes and sevens, for the tired ones were weeping, as we weep now with them. O ! O ! O ! par la pluie ! . . . Then Nuvoletta reflected for the last time in her little long life and she made up all her myriads of drifting minds in one. She cancelled all her engauzements ; she gave a childy cloudy cry : Nuée ! Nuée ! Nuée ! A lightdress fluttered. She was gone."

Note.—" Lightdress : " a concentration, fusion, of light and of nightdress ; " sixteen shimmers : " summers and light ; " Sfumastelliacinous hair : " spray, smoke, stars ; " Dorminant Echo : " sleeping, and dominant.

How beautiful is the whole passage quoted above, and how significant. Here, again, is a passage from " Work in Progress " :

" To sum, horns pew notus pew eurus pew zipher. Ace, deuce, tricks, quarts, quims. While on the other hand, sexes, suppers, oglers, novels and dice. What signifieth all that but 'tis as strange to relate he, nonparile to reed, rite and reckan, caught allmeals dull marks for his nucleud and algobrew. O them dodd-hunters and allanights bate him up jerrybly ! Show that the median interecting at roide angles the legs of a given obtuse one biscuts both the arcs that are subtendered behind."

This passage about adolescence needs, I think, no explanation, nor do the three following phrases, which occur in the same instalment :

" That's a goosey ganswer you're forgivingme,

he is told, what the Deva would you do that
for."

" All in applepine erdor."

" He would smilabit eggways ned, he would, so
prim, and pick upon his ten ordinailed ungles."

Miss Stein's experiments and the results obtained
by these, are of a different order.

In the following example, " Susie Asado," she
produces before our eyes a woman with a canary-
like brightness of disposition, a care for household
matters, a light high voice, and a rather gay slip-
shodness, by the means of rhythm alone. The
reiteration of the word " sweet " recalls a canary's
song :

" Sweet sweet sweet sweet sweet tea.
                    Susie Asado.
Sweet sweet sweet sweet sweet tea.
                    Susie Asado.
Susie Asado which is a told tray sure.
A lean on the shoe this means slips slips hers.
When the ancient light grey is clean it is yellow,
        it is a silver seller.
This is a please this is a please there are the saids
        to jelly. These are the wets these say the
        sets to leave a crown to Incy.
                    Incy is short for incubus.
                    A pot. A pot is a beginning of a
                    rare bit of trees.
Trees tremble, the old vats are in bobbles, bobbles
        which shade and shove and render clean,
        render clean must.

> Drink pups.
> Drink pups drink pups lease a sash hold,
> See it shine and a bobolink has pins. It shows
>   a nail.
>> What is a nail. A nail is unison.
>> Sweet sweet sweet sweet sweet tea."

In this passage we are given the impression, and it is conveyed by the means of rhythm alone—I do not pretend to explain it—that the flying shadows are very fleet, very light.

Miss Stein's power over rhythm is of an extraordinary complexity and subtlety, and by the means of rhythm she conveys all the different shades of character in the persons she evolves before our eyes : the firmness of will or the hesitations, the sweetness and lightness of disposition, or the grace. She conveys by this means, also, the feeling of heat or of cold, and all the minutely subtle distinctions of these, the depth or the fleeting characters of shadows (flying like swallows, deepening into death's coldness) in which the characters move, as well as the nature of their movements, and the sound of their voice.

Here is a passage from " The Portrait of Constance Fletcher."

" Oh the bells that are the same are not stirring and the languid grace is not out of place and the older fur is disappearing. There is not such an end. If it had happened that the little flower was larger and the white colour was deeper and the silent light was darker and the passage was rougher, it would have been as it was and the triumph was in the

place where the light was bright and the beauty
was not having that possession. That was not
what was tenderly. This was the piece of the
health that was strange when there was the dis-
appearance that had not any origin. The darkness
was not the same. There was the uniting and the
preparation that was pleasing and succeeding and
being enterprising. It was not subdued when there
was discussion, it was done when there was the
room that was not a dream."

This passage, down to and inclusive of, the
phrase " The darkness was not the same," revives
in the present writer's consciousness, memories of
a forest in the month of February ; after that there
is, I think, a meeting between friends ; but it is the
pattern, the rhythm, and the texture of the passage
that is important, and through them, the strange
atmosphere that is evoked, and not the story,
not the actual facts.

The French character is conjured up for us
(its love of comfort, of detail, of tidiness, of crowds ;
its practical nature, its lightness, its love of noise)
in the following passage from " France," very
amusingly, beautifully, and with an extraordinary
subtlety. If we try to explain the passage, however,
and to put it into ordinary terms, the magic goes :

" Just a word to show a kite that clouds are
higher than a thing that is smaller, just that word
and no single silence is closer.

" Suggest that the passage is filled with feathers,
suggest that these are all together, suggest that
using boxes is heavy, suggest that there is no

feather, suggest all these things and what is the
result, the result is that everything gets put away.

" All the silence is adequate to a rumble and
all the silliness is adequate to a procession and all
the recitation is equal to the hammer and all the
paving is equal to summer. All the same the
detaining most is the reason that there is a pillar
and mostly what is shocking is a rooster. This is
not so easily said. There is no occasion for a
red result.

" Laugh, to laugh, all the same the tittle is
inclinable. What a change from any yesterday.

" A period of singular results and no gloom such
a period shows such a rapid approach that there is
no search in silence and yet not a sound, not any
sound is searching, no sound is an occasion."

The following passage, from " In the Grass "
(" On Spain ") is even less difficult to follow :
the " story " should, I think, be obvious to all
readers :

" Clambering from a little sea, clambering within
bathing, clambering with a necessary rest for
eyeglasses, clambering beside. A little green is
only seen when they mean to be holder, holder
why, coal pepper is a tissue.

" Come up shot come up cousin come up cold
salmon pearly, come up, come in, nicely, nicely
seen, singing, singing with music, sudden leaves
loaves and turtles, taught turtles taught turtles
teach hot and cold and little drinks."

Here we have not only the friendliness of the
people who are spreading their lunch upon the

fresh green grass, but also, in the sound of "sudden
leaves loaves and turtles, taught turtles taught
turtles " the echo of the wood doves' voices, the
freshness of these.

It may amuse admirers of " The Autobiography
of Alice B. Toklas " to know that there is interior
evidence to show that this lady was at the picnic :
for we find this paragraph is not only in the
rhythm of her speech, but is prefaced by a phrase
much used by her when talking to Miss Stein.
It shows, too, the nature of her practicality.

" Naturally lovey naturally a period which is
regulated by a perfect beam of carpet and more
boats does mean something. It is enough."

As a matter of fact, Miss Stein is, I think, rarely
difficult as to her meanings, for she does not give
us a logical chain of events, she gives us a state of
being ; heat as it really is, shadow as it really is :

" I have thought very much about heat. When
it is really hot one does not go about in the day time.
It is just as well to drink water and even to buy
water if it is necessary. So many people diminish.
And flowers oh how can flowers be north. They
are in the air."

[" So many people diminish." Think of the
shadows cast by people in the heat of noon.]

" In spite of a day a day lost in the heat a day
lost in the heat of the hall, in spite of the day lost
in all the heat we know, in spite of words of surprise
in spite of mats and strawberries in the woods, how

prettily I have taught you to say ' the woods—
the poor man's overcoat ! ' "

In this, amidst the heat, dark shades are cast
by the dark vowels of such words as " lost," " know,"
" hall," " strawberries," " woods "—the last word
being sharper and fresher than the rest.

Miss Stein gives us, nearly always, visual
impressions so terrifyingly sharp that all our present
surroundings are abolished. We know, for instance,
the little girl in " Sacred Emily "—although we
do not know whence she comes—or where she is
going—as well as we know our own childhood :

> " A coral neck and a little song so very extra so
>   very Susie.
> Cow come out cow come out and out and smell
>   a little.
> > Draw prettily.
> > Next to a bloom.
> > Neat stretch.
> > Place plenty.
> > Cauliflower.
> > Cauliflower.
> > Curtain cousin.
> > Apron.
> > Neither best set.
> > Do I make faces like that at you.
> > Pinkie."

In this, a little girl with a neck coral from the sun,
a large sweet clean cow, the little girl's clean bunchy
frock, bunchy as a cauliflower, and a summer
afternoon spent with relations in the country many,

many years ago—all these are transfixed for us, for
eternity.

To me, those lines have an extraordinary visual
beauty, and so have these, from " Scenes " :

" A pale rose is a smell that has no fountain, that
has upside down the same distinction, elegance is
not coloured, the pain is there."

And so have these, from " France " :

" A cloud of white and a chorus of all bright birds
and a sweet a very sweet cherry, a thick miss, a
thick and a dark and a clean clerk, a whole succession
of mantelpieces."

It is no use, however, to charter an omnibus in
order to visit Miss Stein's Olympus.   These are the
days of aeroplanes.

Mr. John Sparrow, a critic of great acuity, and
one who is not enchanted by cheap novelties, has
said (in " Sense and Poetry ") that " Those who
discarded words with their function of reference
and did not attempt to identify and label the items
which went to make up their experience, still less
to abstract from that experience and indicate an
intelligible connection between the abstractions,
might claim that only by thus renouncing intellect
could they achieve their aim in its entirety.

"It seems possible to trace some such endeavour
in the utterances of the Dadaists and Surréalistes,
the latest inheritors of Symbolist tradition.   But
their efforts have lain chiefly in other fields than
literature, for words with all intelligible content,
all meaning and reference knocked out of them are,
to say the least, unattractive symbols, and

o

' literature ' composed of such elements has apparently offered even less hope of communication than analogous travesties of music, painting and sculpture. . . ." Mr. Sparrow continues thus : " Suggestion, evocation of feeling, may none the less effect communications of a sort. . . . It is possible to recognize and share another's mood without the intervention of intelligible speech."

This is true. But the mood must, to be communicated, have reality. And some sensual impression, of pleasure or of pain, should, surely, be conveyed. Mr. Sparrow quotes an example of the failure to communicate anything whatsoever, in " Sense and Poetry." The extract is taken from Mr. George Reavy's " To Icarus."

> " Volutes of molumn whorl
>   toward daos
> Abra cadr (a) is
>   mnemonic lozenge
> To thy foal's limple doubt
>   song unresolved
> From Egypt Daedalus unfurl
> past glowgold sluices of the Sun
> Flown focus grown slowson palpate
> Vulnerable to his firm feel."

We are a patient people. But less patient, perhaps, than are the Americans, who will put up with simply anything—if it is dressed up sufficiently.

CHAPTER IX

ENVOI

In the first chapter of this book, we saw the faint but significant and sinister foreshadowing of the blind, dumb, numb and savourless world into which we now enter. The breath of that world has spread, muffling and fog-like, into the work of the latest school of poets—the unsensed life of a world in which only one sense persists, that of rhythm—a world in which there is some faint perception of where darkness ends and the first faint light begins (and in this it resembles the world when life began)—but which has lost that even earlier perception of the difference between heat and cold. This was the earliest sense (one not yet apprehended) of life. Yet even that early primitive sense is lost to most of the members of the latest school of poetry. This is a greater loss than they realize, since it means for an artist a loss of sensibility for his medium. This perception of heat and cold does not confine itself to physical things in the artist—no matter what his medium may be—but lifted by him into the ideal world of his inspiration, it shows itself in an instinctive feeling for warmth of colour in the actual handling of his medium. Stultification and ultimate degradation of the senses, leads to the loss of one of the most important points of contact between the artist and that world which lies concealed beneath the external physical world ; and this stultification is the result of a spiritual state which, most unfortunately for poetry, is admired and upheld by present critical standards.

We have passed over the brink of the new age, the Machine Age, which is the most enormous upheaval of the physical and spiritual world since the Ice Age, the Iron Age . . . indeed, in this present huge phantasmagoria, we see the phantoms of those ages once again, for this is the Ice Age of the spirit. Not only will the character of the world we live in be changed, but man will become a different animal. He is changing the nature of the power and sensitiveness of his hands, of his sense of touch. Machines are replacing for him his tactile sense, they come between him and the world of touch. And if we consider the difference in intelligence and memory between the elephant and ape, who possess the power of lifting and of handling, and those animals which do not possess this power, we may gain some idea of the future of mankind.

Helvetius [*Note.*—Quoted from Mr. Edgell Richward's " Rimbaud, the Boy and the Poet "] formed the conception of the mind as the product of the senses. Even memory, Helvetius demonstrated, is simply a continuation of sensation, weakened but conserved, so that the mind, whether in itself it be material or not, is completely the product of the nervous sensibility. . . . One of the examples chosen by Helvetius to illustrate his theory is the low mentality of animals, such as the horse. The extremities of these creatures, their

hoofs, are covered with insensitive horn, and if we
consider how much knowledge we owe to the
delicacy of our hands, the reasoning of Helvetius
appears most possible. This, I imagine, was the
starting point of Helvetius' reasoning, if so instant a
step may be called reasoning : " Let us refine our
fingers, that is, all our points of contact with the
exterior world, and our minds will become propor-
tionately superior to those of ordinary men, as theirs
are now to horses." So much for the tactile sense.

The younger poets have the appearance of wishing
to turn themselves into recording machines (though
they have not the extreme sensitiveness of these),
and although I imagine they would deny any
connection with the Surréalistes, the following
phrase, taken from a Surréaliste manifesto, might
well be held to apply to them :

" We," says the manifesto, " have not given
ourselves up to any act of filtration ; in our works
we have made ourselves the deep receptacles of
many echoes, the modern recording apparatuses
which are not hypnotised by the design they record."

In these latest poets, with the exception of Mr.
Spender (who is not of this school) [*Note.*—I hope
to write of Mr. Spender in a later volume, for he
does not come within the scope of my present
argument], the visual sense is almost as non-existent
as in the machines which inhabit their world. Nor
are the unclearly seen objects which break, from
time to time, through the mists that surround them,
apprehended. Here is no act of filtration. We
find in several of these young men, in Mr. Auden
and Mr. Bottrall especially, considerable technical

achievement, as far as rhythmical impetus and the suitability of the rhythm to the theme is concerned, but no tactile sense whatever. The line, in consequence, has neither height nor depth. An intellectual apprehension of words, this they have, but no sensual feeling, no tactile apprehension of them. They do not realize words as entities, rather as birds and beasts are entities, having each their own natural plumage, fur, or hair, of varying thickness and varying colour, of varying surface, softness or roughness. They seem only to prefer one word to another which would have expressed much the same thought, ir that word is useful to the outward pattern.

With these poets, for the most part, we find language used as a separate, debilitated, and necessary but uninteresting covering for the meaning of the poem. On this subject De Quincey, in his essay on " Style," says : " His (Wordsworth's) remark was by far the weightiest thing one ever heard on the subject of style ; and it was this : that it is in the highest degree unphilosophic to call language or diction ' the dress of thoughts. He would call it the incarnation of thoughts.' Never in one word was so profound a truth conveyed, and the truth is apparent on consideration, for if language were merely a dress, then you could lay the thoughts on the left hand, the language on the right. But, generally speaking, you can no more deal thus with poetic thoughts than you can with soul and body. The union is too subtle, the intertexture too ineffable."

The admirers of these poets claim that they

should hold our attention on account of their newness. But *are* they new ? In theme and in abhorrence of the poetical they resemble the flatter figureheads of the Georgian school of poetry, and such poets as Emerson and Matthew Arnold— but without their modesty. They have, however, substituted new clichés for old, and clichés that are of a more temporary character than the clichés of Emerson. In them indeed, as a whole, we find the same fault as that of which Lawrence accused Mr. Joyce : " old and hard-worked staleness masquerading as the all-new." All, or nearly all, of these poets present surface difficulties, because they suppress intermediary processes of thought, or else they give so many that the reader is bewildered. This surface difficulty gives the average person the impression that the poems conceal great depths. But this is rarely so.

Let us consider the themes which are usual to this poetry. This is the age when we hear the sounds of the tapping from the tombs, and of the million hammers that shall rebuild the dawn, breaking through the small disastrous whispering sounds of the dust as it gathers itself in one final effort to overwhelm the spirit.

We have come to the age of the steel men, and of factories that sing in the place of birds, and, we must, therefore, have rhythms that are necessary to the needs of the time. But it must be remembered that great poetry of every age is a logical development in theme and manner upon the poetry of the past ; therefore, when we speak of innovations in technique, it would, perhaps, as

Mr. Eliot has pointed out, be better to say
" developments."

All subjects are suitable to poetry, if they are
sublimated and sifted through the poet's experience.
The movements of common life, dream, heroic
action, wisdom, passion, experience and innocence,
these are the natives of poetry, with everything
which can ennoble delight, comfort, or fire the
soul of man, increase the consciousness of the
race, or give us new sense-values. " The functions
of the poetical faculty," said Shelley, " are twofold ;
by one it creates new materials of knowledge and
power and pleasure ; by the other it engenders
in the mind a desire to reproduce and arrange
them according to a certain rhythm and order
which may be called the beautiful and the good."
I do not find this creation, this reproduction and
arrangement, in much of the latest output of verse.
It is impossible also, to deny that certain critics
of the art wish to confine the subjects of poetry
to a kind of Marxian treatise, varied by auto-
biographical passages, the key to which is lost
in the mind of the writer. Most of these poems
are personal without possessing personality ; they
are nearly all indistinguishable from each other.
Most of these poets, Miss Laura Riding, for instance,
might exchange their signature for another without
anyone being the wiser. These poems deal with
personal situations, yet they have not been passed
through the experience in such a way as to show that
power of which Coleridge speaks, of " reducing
multitude into a unity of effect and modifying
a series of thoughts by one predominant thought

or feeling." Yet it is only by this process of assimilating and giving out again, that we can reject what is superfluous, untrue, or half true. The process of assimilation is rare amongst these poets, as we shall see from the following poem by Mr. Herbert Read:

THE INNOCENT EYE.

" The potential
    mirror of gentle acts
    agent of factual
    joy
    enjoy
    deft enquiry
    but shade yourself
    against electric signs

    Angelicos
    diatoms
    of senseful surfeit
    How can man deny you ?

    He should employ you
    whenever
    he wakes in the world
    out of dusty fever

    And with not worm
    and weevil
    for whom
    God grows staveacre

    But with bird and lynx
    enlarge his life
    with crystal lens
    and furtive lust."

Note.—Quoted from " Sense and Poetry," by John Sparrow.

234 ASPECTS OF MODERN POETRY

It seems to me that nothing has been assimilated, nothing rejected, in this poem ; multitude has not been reduced into unity of effect. The rhythm is, as a result, flaccid and unmeaning. It has no impetus, and is unrelated to the meaning of the poem. It is a fact that certain poets of today, occupied with implicit meanings which have their own value but are unrelated to the necessities of poetry, or occupied with their own personal reactions to certain personal situations, distract us with little broken miniature mirrors of a thousand different worlds, all completely unrelated (though brought together in one poem), and not co-ordinated. The inevitable result is not only distraction but loss of outline, and, in some cases, loss of rhythmical impetus. We can see the loss of rhythmical impetus in the poem quoted above. The rhythm, such as it is (and it scarcely exists, it is entirely unliving), is completely meaningless ; it has no relation to the theme. Any other rhythm could have taken its place. Nor has the texture any meaning ; this, again, is not only unpleasing because it is flaccid but is unrelated to the theme.

My complaint against a certain number of the poets mentioned in this chapter is not that their poems are ugly, even though it cannot be claimed that they are beautiful ; nor do I complain that they are unaccustomed (my own poems, in their time, have had both these charges brought against them). My complaint is that they are almost invariably dull to an unprecedented degree, platitudinous and numb-fingered. They leave a sense

of hopeless fatigue in the mind, and this is not
because they cause us to exercise our minds with
too great vigour, but because they swaddle our
minds with cotton-wool, with an unliving substance,
at once deadening and unresisting.

The claim is brought forward, on behalf of these
poets, that in using ordinary speech-rhythms,
ordinary or " unpoetical " words, and ordinary
episodes of life, they are producing something new
in poetry. But how can this be so when Chaucer,
Crabbe and Hood used the ordinary episodes of
life as themes, when Wordsworth claimed the
right for a poet to use the common speech of life.
With Wordsworth we find ourselves in an everyday
world made splendid by the light of a genius which
illuminates but does not transform the objects of
that life. Common speech and common experience
are here, but all made radiant and unforgettable by
inspiration. The ordinary objects of life attain
supernatural qualities, and yet they are the objects
which we have always seen and have never understood ; the common celandine is still the common
celandine, but it is also a star. With most of the
younger poets who are writing today, this is not so.
We are given a description of life, but not life itself.
Whilst making a great show of creating, or at any
rate explaining, a new world, they produce entirely
meaningless chatter heard in omnibus, tram or
butcher's shop, arising from nothing, leading to
nothing, illuminating nothing and transmuting
nothing—neither the state of the world, nor
the state of the individual soul. Their
poems are neither co-ordinated so as to make

a pattern, nor sublimated so as to add to our
experience.

Consider the difference between certain of these
poems, and Mr. Eliot's " Waste Land," in which
each phrase heard in the street is endued suddenly,
with a terrible meaning, speaks, suddenly, " above
a mortal mouth," is transmuted, because of
the genius which illuminates it, to the Writing
on the Wall—a monument for all time, pointing
to the futility of the modern world.

" HURRY UP PLEASE IT'S TIME
HURRY UP PLEASE IT'S TIME
Goonight Bill. Goonight Lou. Goonight May.
Goonight.
Ta ta. Goonight. Goonight.
Good night, ladies, good night, sweet ladies,
good night, good night."

(Time for the world to end. Time for this
" handful of dust " to hurry to its last bed.) This
is the sound that the people hear as they stumble
from the public house. But is it that alone ? Is
not the last line an echo from some vast tragedy of
indecision—an echo which mimics only too closely
the general tragedy of this world ? How far removed
is the terrible poignant sweetness of the last line
from the mouth from which it now sounds. " Good
night, sweet ladies, good night, good night." Here
we have the dying world, fading into the universal
darkness.

Consider again, these lines from Mr. Ezra Pound's
" Thirty Cantos."

" Life to make mock of motion :
For the husks, before me, move,
The words rattle : shells given out by shells.
The live man, out of lands and prisons,
         shakes the dry pods,
Probes for old wills and friendships, and the big
      locust-casques
Bend to the tawdry table,
Lift up their spoons to mouths, put forks in
      cutlets,
And makes sound like the sound of voices."

This is less great poetry than the " Waste Land,"
but still it is a real experience, transmuted into
poignant and true poetry. But what are we to
make of this extract from Mr. Louis Zukofsky's
very long poem " From A," which appeared in
Mr. Pound's " Active Anthology " ? (The rest of
the poem is on about the same level.)

" And it was to the glory of Liza-Arcy's
And Eliza Jane (her kids : ' here lies a jane !')
         his friend's wife who came only on invitation ;
That they walked only with their hubbies—
Two individual families,
Having taken over standards that would
Have been impoliteness to Eskimos.

Seriously : as serious as
Four and a half decades kiddin' himself on a
      minature golf course.

But I tell you this man had vistas :
Ties, handkerchiefs to watch,
Mufflers, dress shirts, golf holes,
Chocolate éclairs, automobiles and entrées.

Played polo.
And they — they — the very old stutterers,
    mumbltypeg in duplex Park Av. apartments,
Mumbling imperceptibly, when the jack-knife
    stuck $25 shoe leather.

Those who were their grandchildren
Who got jobs because ' They didn't believe in
    Santa Claus,'
Said Henry, ' good boys, Unk Magnus, they come
    of good families.' "

What illumination does this throw on ordinary
life ? None. It is however, only fair to Mr.
Zukofsky to say that the poem, when taken as a
whole, has some rhythmical impetus ; and we find
this in most of the younger poets. Yet, strangely
enough, in nearly all cases, this merely produces in
our mind the impression that they are *running away
from something.*

Let us take the example of Mr. Auden. This
young poet's rhythms almost invariably produce
this sensation of running away, and the rhythms, are,
in all cases, the result of outward structure alone.
The words lie dead on the page.

Mr. Auden has an able mind, but, unhappily,
he writes uninteresting poetry, or, at least, his poetry
nearly always lacks interest. When therefore, we
are told by an admiring reviewer that, since the
publication of his first volume, two or three years
ago, " it has been generally recognized that he is
one of the four or five living poets worth quarrelling
about "—and that " Here is something as important

as the appearance of Mr. Eliot's poems fifteen years ago "—I can only reply that this is sheer nonsense. Mr. Eliot's poems, from the very beginning, showed signs of that genius which fires and ennobles his work—had always, too, an integral being, an intense visual and tactile sense, had depth, wisdom and passion.

The meaning of Mr. Auden's poems is frequently so obscure that it defies detection, and, it is this obscurity, I imagine, which has frightened certain timid critics into this excessive admiration. He is unfortunate, inasmuch as a great deal of nonsense is talked about his work, and that his most fervent admirers contradict each other about his aims. A usually intelligent reviewer, for instance, explained to us that " The Orators " " is quite definitely not a book to be apprehended intellectually. . . . Read as passively as possible, just a body sensitized to words, without letting intellect interfere. . . . Don't bother to think at first, just listen. Then it will all begin to stand out like the red Cliffs of Parnassos. . . ." Another critic, however, announces that " here is thought stripped to its essentials." My own impression is that Mr. Auden has a real capacity for feeling, and considerable rhythmical sense, but that he is too apt to be carried away by the necessities of pattern-making, and that these patterns are superimposed on the material ; they are, as well, oral alone, and have nothing to do with the visual sense.

Mr. Auden's greatest danger, in his longer poems, is that he is led towards disintegration, not cohesion, of matter and of manner. A certain critic said of

him that " We must wonder if Book II, the ' Journal
of an Airman,' is perhaps a kind of life of Lawrence,
reduced to elements and then built up again." I
find that whereas Mr. Auden frequently reduces
his subject to fragments, he does not always reduce
them to elements (the latter being at times a
valuable process). Still less often does he rebuild
the fragments. Mr. Auden does not organize his
experience. It must be said, too, that his material
is too often of a purely temporary interest, has no
universal significance. And in this failure to sift,
and then reorganize the experience, lies one of the
major dangers of the poetry of our time. It is
especially Mr. Auden's danger. In the power of
assimilating details into a whole, in the visual and
the tactile sense, Mr. Auden is, at the moment,
almost entirely lacking. " The Orators," for
instance, is not an organic whole. It may be claimed
that it represents the disintegration of the world
in its present state, but it shows merely lack of fusion,
looseness of interest, " the belief," to quote Mr.
John Sparrow, " that experience hitherto taken to
be the raw material of art, should be accepted as
its finished product."

Here then, in Mr. Auden, we have the raw
material of art ; and sometimes, but very rarely,
the finished product.

What interest, for instance, can this passage, which
occurs on page 66 of " The Orators," arouse in the
mind of the reader :

" I'm afraid it sounds more like a fairy story
      There was a family called Do ;

There were Do-a, Do-ee, and other Do-s
And Uncle Dick and Uncle Wiz had come to
    stay with them
(Nobody slept that night.)
Now Do-a loved to bathe before his breakfast
With Uncle Dick, but Uncle Wiz . . .
Well ?
As a matter of fact the farm was in Pembrokeshire,
The week the Labour Cabinet resigned.
Dick had returned from Germany in love.
I hate cold water and am very fond of potatoes.
You're wondering about these scratches ? "

I am not ! I am wondering at the simple
credulity of the critics and the public in allowing
themselves to be gulled by such unattractive
nonsense. We can see, in the following lines, how
much the absence of the visual sense, and the
tactual sense, affects, to its detriment, Mr. Auden's
poetry. This poem (I cannot quote it in its
entirety) is admirably formed, as far as structure
goes ; the last (unquoted) verse brings it to a
perfect whole as far as thought and movement and
climax are concerned, but the absence of the
visual and tactual senses, of any delight in physical
beauty, renders the poem tasteless in the sense in
which food cooked without salt is tasteless.

"From the very first coming down
  Into a new valley with a frown
  Because of the sun and a lost way,
  You certainly remain : to-day
  I, crouching behind a sheep-pen, heard
  Travel across a sudden bird,

P

Cry out against the storm, and found
The year's arc a completed round
And love's worn circuit re-begun,
Endless with no dissenting turn.
Shall see, shall pass, as we have seen
The swallow on the tile, spring's green
Preliminary shiver, passed
A solitary truck, the last
Of shunting in the Autumn, But now
To interrupt the homely brow,
Thought warmed to evening through and
    through
Your letter comes, speaking as you,
Speaking of much but not to come."

Here indeed is a blind world, a world in which
the objects would not taste if we put them to our
mouths, or smell if we held them to our noses.
Is this a poetry of pure thought ?   If so, can it be
claimed that the thought is of any value in this case ?

In spite of these great disadvantages, however,
Mr. Auden's poems do, at moments, express a very
real and poignant emotion, and the body he chooses
for his expression is on these occasions adequate and
moving.   Take, for instance, this passage from
" Paid on Both Sides " :

" Always the following wind of history
Of others' wisdom makes a buoyant air
Till we come suddenly on pockets where
Is nothing loud but us ; where voices seem
Abrupt, untrained, competing with no lie
Our fathers shouted once.   They taught us war,
To scamper after darlings, to climb hills

To emigrate from weakness, find ourselves
The easy conquerors of empty bays :
But never told us this, left each to learn,
Hear something of that soon-arriving day
When to gaze longer and delighted on
A face or idea be impossible.
Could I have been some simpleton that lived
Before disaster sent his runners here ;
Younger than worms, worms have too much to
    bear.
Yes, mineral were best : could I but see
These woods, these fields of green, this lively
    world
Sterile as moon."

This fragment, until the tragic expressiveness of
the last six lines, has a phrasing, a texture, a diction,
which are deliberately threadbare and flat to suit
this wearied and hopeless dirge for an outworn
world. We can compare this purposeful thread-
bareness and flatness, so suitable to the theme and
to the emotion expressed, with the unsuitable flat
threadbare texture of " The Shropshire Lad,"
where the theme is usually eager and believing
youth brought to disaster by circumstances, and
with the knowledge that death lies at the end of
the road, yet keeping his soul undimmed and
unstained.

The lines which I have quoted from Mr. Auden
are followed by the controlled passion, underlying,
yet not breaking through the lines of this passage :

" . . . The body warm but not
By choice, he dreams of folk in dancing bunches,

Of tart wine spilt on home-made benches,
Where learns, one drawn apart, a secret will
Restore the dead ; but comes thence to a wall.
Outside on frozen soil lie armies killed
Who seem familiar but they are cold."

The technique used in this, though purposely
less heavy and less magnificent in diction and
texture than the following poem by Wilfred Owen,
is the same ; he ends his lines with falling or rising
dissonances instead of rhymes. I quote the shorter
version of Owen's poem (" Strange Meeting ") :

" Earth's wheels run oiled with blood.   Forget we
        that.
Let us lie down and dig ourselves in thought.
Beauty is yours and you have mastery,
Wisdom is mine, and I have mystery.
We two will stay behind and keep our troth.
Let us forego men's minds that are brutes'
        natures,
Let us not sup the blood which some say nurtures,
Be we not swift with swiftness of the tigress.
Let us break ranks from those who trek from
        progress.
Miss we the march of this retreating world
Into old citadels that are not walled.
Let us lie out and hold the open truth,
Then when their blood hath clogged the chariot
        wheels
We will go up and wash them from deep wells,
What though we sink from men as pitchers falling
Many shall raise us up to be their filling

Even from wells we sunk too deep for war
And filled by brows that bled where no wounds
were."

Owen's great poem has exerted much influence
over modern technique, and we find Mr. Auden
using this device of ending the line with dissonances,
over and over again.

Now let us take the case of Mr. Cecil Day Lewis.
Here is a young poet with a certain spiritual vision.
In him, again, the bodily visual sense and the
tactual sense are lacking; but I imagine this
avoidance is partly (though not wholly) voluntary.
He regards the intrusion of physically sensual life
as dangerous. The physical world is his enemy,
imperilling his spiritual vision.

We can see how strong is that avoidance, in
these poignantly felt and impressive lines :

" Nearing again the legendary isle
Where sirens sang and mariners were skinned
We wonder now what was there to beguile
That such stout fellows left their bones behind.

These chorus-girls are surely past their prime,
Voices grow shrill and paint is wearing thin,
Lips that sealed up the sense from gnawing time
Now beg the favour with a graveyard grin.

We have no flesh to spare and they can't bite,
Hunger and sweat have stripped us to the bone ;
A skeleton crew we toil upon the tide
And mock the theme-song meant to lure us on :

No need to stop the ears, avert the eyes
From purple rhetoric of evening skies."

The last two lines of the second quatrain are, to
my feeling, good poetry; the third quatrain is good,
the following couplet definitely bad.

Mr. Day Lewis' poems are, in nearly every case
truthful, bare and austere; they are born from
controlled spiritual passion, as we can see from the
following lines from the " Magnetic Mountain " :

" But Two there are, shadow us everywhere
    And will not let us be till we are dead,
    Hardening our bones, keeping the spirit spare,
    Original in water, earth and air,
    Our bitter cordial, our daily bread.

    .   .   .   .   .

    Such are the temporal princes, fear and pain,
    Whose borders march with the ice-fields of death,
    And from that servitude escape there's none
    Till in the grave we set up house alone
    And buy our liberty with our last breath."

" Till in the grave we set up house alone " is
probably an unconscious echo from a verse by that
extremely bad poet Emily Dickinson, but Mr.
Day Lewis has transmuted it into really fine poetry.

How dead, then, is the material world which
Mr. Day Lewis sees around him—a world of
shadows governed by Time. Even the pulse in
the heart has changed, in this world, to the beat
of Time; has become a world of mathematical
units :

" Ours the curriculum
    Neither of building birds nor wasteful waters,

Bound in book not violent in vein :
Here we inoculate with dead ideas
Against blood-epidemics, against
The infection of faith and the excess of life.
Our methods are up to date ; we teach
Through head and not by heart,
Language with gramophones and sex with charts,
Prophecy by deduction, prayer by numbers.
For honours see prospectus : those who leave us
Will get a post and pity the poor ;
Their eyes glaze at strangeness ;
They are never embarrassed, have a word for
    everything,
Living on credit, dying when the heart stops ;
Will wear black armlets and stand a moment in
    silence
For the passing of an era, at their own funeral."

The material of this is both interesting and well
thought out, but it cannot be claimed that it is
good poetry. It is far inferior to the two other
passages I have quoted, with the exception of the
really fine and significant phrase " dying when the
heart stops." In the avoidance of physical beauty,
which we see in this passage, an avoidance which is
perhaps, at this time, a necessity for him, lies Mr.
Day Lewis' danger. It is to be hoped that in the
future, when the spiritual life is assured to him in
such a way that he does not fear that it will fade,
this young poet will become on terms of friendship
with this other world which lies around us, whose
radiance, whose fleeting colours, gleams and sounds,
all bear their message from another life.

Mr. Ronald Bottrall is another young poet with an interesting mind, a considerable gift for fluency and cohesion of rhythm (his rhythms are never superimposed), and no tactile or visual sense whatever. He has, however, a lesser gift for bareness of statement than that possessed by Mr. Day Lewis, and his poetry, therefore, makes less effect. Yet it has a moving quality when it is at its best. But I am still left with the feeling that Mr. Bottrall is an extremely intelligent young man who will make his influence felt in some other sphere than that of poetry or that, in any case, he has not yet found himself as a poet. The following lines, taken from " The Future is not for us " (" The Loosening and other Poems," the Minority Press), show both his qualities and his faults :

" The future is not for us, though we can set up
    Our barriers, rest in our dead-embered
    Sphere, till we come to pause over our last loving-
        cup
    With death. We are dismembered
    Into a myriad broken shadows,
    Each to himself reflected in a splinter of that glass
    Which we once knew as cosmos, and the close
    Of our long progress is hinted by the crass
    Fogs creeping slow and darkly
    From out the middle west. We can humanize,
    We can build new temples for the body,
    Set our intellect to tilt against the spies
    Of fortune, call this Chance or that Fate,
    Estimate the logical worth of ' it may depend.'. ..
    But we know that we are at the gate

Leading out of the path
Which was to be an Amen having neither
beginning nor end."

This is finely thought out, and, if we consider
the meaning alone, it is fine poetry ; but, unhappily,
in poetry the soul is not of much use without the
body. And what are we to make, from a technical
point of view, of such lines as these :

" Which we once knew as cosmos, and the close
Of our long progress is hinted by the crass."

Here we have a technical echo of Mr. Empson's
lines, quoted at the end of the essay on Hopkins :

" Your part is of earth's surface and mass the same
Of all Cosmos' volume, and all stars as well."

Both Mr. Bottrall and Mr. Empson ought to
learn to " kick the geese out of the boat," to quote
an expression of Tennyson's. But this is not the
only trouble in these lines. The thick muddy
vowel-sounds add unpleasantness to the already
unpleasing slow-dragging, cloying, and pointless
scheme of S's. If the poets are intending to
produce the impression of primeval slime, they do
not do so. Their mud is ordinary, if thick, mud.

Here is another specimen from Mr. Bottrall
which for me has a moving quality, and in which
the movement is suited to the theme :

" There is yet time, even though the clock
Is set, there is yet time to brave
The annals of our age, to put our ' wave
Of progress ' in its proper place, recant

Our late betrayal and plant
Within the shadow of the rock
Our bloodless bodies.   Ask, ask.   Yet
There is time to break the barricadoes hard
Hammered against the looked-for synthesis,
To discard our Chaplin-hero
In child-lost-like myopic round
Beating against the legs of a giant Talus in an
    iron mask,
Avoiding hardly the automatic strokes
Dealt by his flail.
Time to call up Eros armed to his new Psychean
    task
Of mobilising moving dunes of grainèd sand
Into an adamantine pyramid
Rising upward, upward."

This fragment is nearly, though not quite,
admirable.   For Mr. Bottrall falls into the faults
of nearly all his contemporaries.   He localizes the
general tragedy in such a way as to dwarf it, as in
the lines :

" To discard our Chaplin-hero
In child-lost-like myopic round
Beating against the legs of a giant Talus in an
    iron mask."

The last line is definitely weak and bad.   The
following passage, from " Arion Anadymenos," is
distinguished by a beautiful and most moving first
line.   From the fifth line on it becomes bathetic :

" Is it worth while to make lips smile again,
To transmit that uneasiness in us which craves

A moment's mouthing, craves to bully the pain
The pain and the pity of it into staves
Of crabbed pothooks, filling the breadth
Of title-page to colophon ?
Is it worth while to debate upon
The automatic sense which forces us
To circumvent our quietus
And put instead on record
Reactions to the vibrations of a vocal chord ? "

This verse has virtue of a kind, rhythmically ;
but for all that it is singularly dead verbally.

All the young poets I have mentioned have
certain mental qualities, but they have not one
touch of genius. Their poems are all " written
on the level," as one might say. If we compare
their work with " Sweeney among the Nightingales,"
with " Sweeney Erect " and with " Whispers of
Immortality," all poems having been written, if my
memory is not at fault, when Mr. Eliot had only
just passed the age of thirty (I have not my first
editions with me, and have no memory for dates),
we shall see the difference. Here we have a man
who has talked with fiery angels, and with angels
of a clear light and holy peace, and who has " walked
amongst the lowest of the dead."

A strange and significant result of the Machine
Age, perhaps unconscious on the part of the writers,
perhaps semi-conscious, is the way in which poets
mutilate, or fill with waste product, the unheard-
rhythms of the blank spaces on a page. Now,
what appear to be the blank spaces on a page—
the space between couplet and couplet, the space

between quatrain and quatrain and, in a minor
way, the space of the margin and, more slightly
still, the space between word and word—all these
apparently bare spaces are filled with unexpressed
rhythm, heard only within the mind—are filled,
as we might say, with the muted beat of time—
only not regular, but moving now slower, now
quicker. This unexpressed rhythm, which is part
of the air in which the poem lives, is now being
destroyed, or in some cases used up, by certain of
the newer poets, in a perfectly arbitrary and, for
the most part, meaningless manner by the cutting
up of words into fragments, of which one fragment,
perhaps, may lie dead at the end of one line, and
the second fragment lie dead at the beginning of
the next. Arising out of no logical necessity from
within the poem, one line will be very long and
the next shrunken. This not only distorts the
body of the poem but, as I have said, it destroys
those unexpressed rhythms which surround the
poem as the air surrounds a living and moving body.

Mr. E. E. Cummings provides us, at moments,
with particularly bad examples of this vice. His
is a strange case, since he varies between writing
unassimilated, shapeless, unbeautiful, unilluminating
and redundant nonsense, and poems which, at
moments, have a form which is beautiful and
inherent in their material.

His vice of destroying the unexpressed rhythms
in a page is shown in his worst work, not only by
puffing out or shrinking lines for no reason, but
also by cutting words into blocks, placing capitals
in the middle of words, intruding long and

meaningless spaces between words, punctuating in
odd places for no reason, and running two or more
words into one, as in this poem :

" inthe,exquisite ;

    morning sure lyHer eye s exactly sit,ata little
        roundtable
    among otherlittle roundtables Her,eyes   count
        slow(ly

    obstre poroustimidi ties surElyfl)oat iNg,the

    ofpieces ofof sunligh tof fa l l in gof throughof
        treesOf.

(Fields Elysian

the like,a)slEEping neck a breathing a ,lies
(slo wlythe wom an pa)ris her
flesh : wakes
               in little streets

while exactlygir lisHlegs;play;ing;nake;D
and

chairs wait under the trees

Fields slowly Elysian in
a firmcool-Ness taxis,sQuirM

and, betw ee nch air st ott er s thesillyold
WomanSellingBaloonS

In theex qui site

morning,
              her sureLyeye s sit-ex actly her
                   sitsat a surely !)little,

     roundtable   amongother;littleexactly   round.
       tables,

  Her

          .eyes"

   This seems to me a very easy and naive way of
covering up nakedness, but I suppose it has impressed
the lads of the village, who imagine that they are
assisting at the creation of the New and the
Important.   In this poem, Mr. Cummings' reason
for cutting up words into separate blocks, running
two or more words into one, placing long spaces
between words or fragments of words, placing
capitals in the middle of words, and punctuating in
odd places, is that he wished to reproduce the
impression of the chattering lights of a summer
morning falling between leaves, then the darkening
as a little air brings the leaves together, and the
sudden space of pure sunlight as the branches are
drawn apart again.   But in spite of this, I submit
that the poem is anything but beautiful ; not only
does it possess, in an acute degree, the vice of which
I have spoken, but the material from which it is
made is ordinary and dull.   If we translate it into
ordinary script, and into prose—for frankly the
outline of the poem is of no account, the rhythmical
beat is non-existent—we find that Mr. Cummings
has given us no new experience, has not illuminated
for us our known experience.
   As far as I can make out (the poem is rendered
additionally obscure by the fact that Mr. Cummings,
from time to time, throws in a word which seems
unrelated to the sense), the poem, plainly written

in prose, would run thus : " In the exquisite
morning, surely her eyes sit at a little round table
among other little round tables ; her eyes count
obstreporous timidities surely floating, the pieces of
sunlight falling through trees ! Like the Elysian
Fields. A sleeping neck breathing, lies slowly the
woman Paris ; her flesh wakes. In little streets
exactly girlish legs playing naked, and chairs wait
under the trees. Fields, slowly Elysian in a firm
coolness ; taxis squirm, and, between chairs, totters
the silly old woman selling balloons. In the
exquisite morning "—and here I come to a pause,
for I cannot elucidate the meaning of

" her sureLyeye s sit-ex actly her
       sitsat a surely."

Perhaps Mr. Cummings is hinting that she surely
sat at a little round table among others ; little
exactly round tables.

What interest does this present to the mind ? It
presents none.

The verse is bad ; but when translated into
the medium of prose, does it make good prose ? It
does not.

The verse produces nothing to claim our attention,
excepting the arbitrary chopping about of words.
We shall be told that this is like life, and that life,
to quote Laforgue, is quotidian. But surely there
must be *some* compensation ? Here there is none.
Nor can it be held that this arbitrary mutilation
and grafting of words is permissible. A poet should
be able to obtain this effect of flickering summer
lights by the means of skilful inter-arrangement of

one-syllabled words with words of two or more
syllables, and by the use of bright, sharp, and not
heavy consonants.

We have found an explanation, though no excuse,
for the mutilations of words and the eccentricities of
the type in the above poem, but in the following, also
by Mr. Cummings, the mutilations and graftings are
not only inexcusable, they are perfectly meaningless.

" Among
            these
                    red pieces of
        day(against which and
        quite silently hills
        made of blueandgreen paper

        scorchbend ingthem
        selves - U
        pcurv E ,into :
                    anguish (clim
        b) ing
        s-p-i-r-a
        l
        and, disappear)
                    Satanic and blasé

        a black goat lookingly wanders

        there is nothing left of the world but
        into this noth
        ing il treno per
        Roma si-gnori ?
        jerk,
        ilyr, ushes."

This is inexcusable.   From the word " scorch-
bend " to " blasé " the writer conveys a series of

false impressions, which are the result of nothing but his arbitrary maltreatment of words. For instance, the letter E, printed separately, as in this poem, is compounded of right angles, and it is a gross æsthetic fault to use it in this way at the end of the word " curve " and immediately before the word " into." What significance has the colon after " into," or the shifting of the word that follows, " anguish," so that there is an empty space at the beginning of the line ? If " anguish " had been the only word in the line, this shifting would have had some significance. As it is, it is merely irritating. Again, an upward-moving spiral does not remain horizontal, so why print the word thus :

     s-p-i-r-a
     l ?

If the writer could not resist the common habit of illustrating the word " spiral " with a physical movement, why did he not print the word thus :

        p   r   l
    S   i   a

It is true that this would be just as boring as his way of doing it, but it would be more accurate, and the apostles of the Machine Age should, above all, observe the verities which belong to machines.

As for the last two lines, descriptive of the running of the Rome express, I can only suggest that at the moment when the poet was observing it, the train was in the act of jumping the points, and that it subsequently went off the rails.

Let us now see what significance *can* be given to these seemingly blank spaces on a page. Here are

Q

a few lines from Mr. Sacheverell Sitwell's " Canons
of Giant Art " :

" This was the morning of Queen Dido's hunt ;
 The Tyrian town, Carthage, din of arms and busy
   harbour
Slept,
     Slept,
          Slept,
               Until Aurora rose,
 Till day lit the seas and touched the snow-capped
   mountains
White,
     Her horses,
          Snowy-white the foam
In the high clear morning."

The prolonging and deepening of oblivion is
produced not only by the recurrence of the word
" slept," but by the actual shifting of the word
on the page, so that there is an empty space beneath
it. This effect of profound and wide-spread sleep
would not have been so completely conveyed if
the three words had been on the same line, or had
stood exactly beneath each other. Again, a definite
impression of change in the quality of colour, of
movement, of texture, and of the ground, is conveyed by the sound and spacing of

" White,
     Her horses,"

following immediately on the static quantity of the
preceding full line, and preceding the gliding
quality and movement of the half-line :

          " Snowy-white the foam."

With this difference held in our minds, let us compare the poems of Mr. Cummings already quoted, with the following two exquisite and flawless little poems by the same author, and we may wonder why, having the sensitive and beautiful talent which he undoubtedly possesses, he should trouble, or condescend, to present us with pretentious façades making an elaborate concealment of emptiness. (There *are* seemingly empty façades which hold realities masquerading as ghosts, but these Mr. Cummings has not given us.)

Here, then, are two exquisite and flawless poems by the author I have blamed because he has departed from his gifts :

" You are like the snow only
  purer fleeter, like the rain
  Only sweeter frailer you

  Whom certain
  flowers ressemble but trembling (cowards
      which fear
  to miss within your least gesture the hurting
  skill which lives) and since

  Nothing lingers
  beyond a little instant,
  along with rhyme and with laughter
  O my lady
  (and every brittle marvelous breathing thing)

  Since i and you are on our ways to dust

  of your fragility
  (but chiefly of your smile,
  most suddenly which is
  of love and death a marriage) you give me

courage
so that against myself
the sharp days slobber in vain :
nor am i afraid that
this, which we call autumn, cleverly
dies and over the ripe world wanders with
a near and careful
smile on his mouth (making
everything suddenly old and with his awkward eyes pushing
sleep under and thoroughly
into all beautiful things)
winter, whom Spring shall kill."

Here there is no profound meaning, but we have, undoubtedly, an exquisitely lovely poem, with a delicate, hesitating, and fluctuating rhythm, like the shape and colourlessness of the first flowers, when winter is about to break into spring. This beauty, this delicate rhythm, this feeling of an early flower scarcely daring to unfold its delicate buds in the cold wind, is obtained, not only by the varying length of the lines, but by the absence of external rhymes coupled with the use of assonances and of an occasional rhyme or dissonance placed with an exquisite delicacy *within* the lines. Let us take the first verse :

> 1   2   2
> " You are like the snow only
> 1   3   4
> purer fleeter, like the rain
> 2   3   4   1
> only sweeter frailer you."

The dissonance of " you," taken in conjunction

with the assonances " snow " and " only," and in
the next line, with the dissonance of " purer,"
these produce a strange, cold, and lovely effect.
The sound of " you " is crisp like the petals of
the earliest flowers ; this sound softens into the
deeper sound of " snow " and of " only." " Purer "
is less crisp than " you," it is also deeper in sound ;
but we have the feeling of petals shrinking together
in the young cold wind which comes between
winter and spring. After the word " rain " comes
its assonance " frailer," which has a little trembling
movement, half imperceptible.

The internal rhymes placed in exactly the same
place in two adjacent lines :

> " Purer *fleeter*, like the rain
> Only *sweeter* frailer you "—

these show us the flower lifting itself up on its
delicate stem, after the early spring shower has passed.

Further on in the poem we have the assonances
of " ressemble " and " trembling " placed in the
same line, and giving, to one reader at least, the
feeling of the pure narrow outline of the flower-bell ;
whilst, in the next verse, the far-removed internal
rhymes of " little " and, three lines after, " brittle "
seems like the faintest green shadow in the delicate
bell-shape, as do the assonances of " nothing lingers."
Then we have the sharp unripe dissonances, like
the unripe cold of early spring, of " marriage " and
the deeper, stronger sound of " courage," and the
high cold assonances of the A sounds in :

> " so that against myself
> the sharp days slobber in vain."

After the first verse a kind of faint and almost imperceptible ground-rhythm is formed by the assonance pattern of unsharp " i's," some accented, some, like the " i's " in " within " and " which," hardly accented at all—a sound which makes us think of a delicate growing thing persisting against the cold, in some half-light, and with that faint green shadow in the heart :

" To miss within your least gesture the hurting
  Skill which lives) and since
  Nothing lingers
  beyond a little instant,
  along with rhyme and with laughter
  O my lady
  (and every brittle marvelous breathing thing)."

This scheme, with the faint sharp " g " sounds which, at moments, give an extra depth and piercingness to the cold, occurs at intervals throughout the rest of the poem, and is varied by a pattern of sharp and poignant " i " sounds, like a gleam of pale and early sunlight.

Here is another poem which is almost equally beautiful, if we except the horrible word " wiggles " :

" After all white horses are in bed

  will you walking beside me, my very lady,
  if scarcely the somewhat city
  wiggles in considerable twilight
  touch (now) with a suddenly unsaid
  gesture lightly my eyes ?
  and send life out of me and the night
  absolutely into me . . . a wise

and puerile moving of your arm will
do suddenly that
                              will do
more than heroes beautifully in shrill
armour colliding on huge blue horses,
and the poets looked at them, and made verses,
through the sharp light cryingly as the knights
flew."

Here again we have a skilful and lovely pattern
of unsharp and of poignant " i " sounds, falling
throughout the poem, but the sense conveyed by
these is necessarily different to that conveyed in
the other poem, because of the different associations.

The feeling that we are walking—so smoothly
that we might be floating—in the summer twilight
through some city of a youthful dream, is the result,
partly, of the smoothness of the double-syllabled
words ending each line of the first tryptych and
the next single line ; whilst the feeling of floating
towards some lovely distance or horizon is produced
by the long " i's " in the words ending three of
the lines in the five-lined verse, echoing, subtly,
the assonantal " i's " in the middle of the first
two lines :

" gesture lightly my eyes
and send life out of me, and the night,"
though " my " and " life " are very lightly
accented, indeed, hardly accented at all.

These long " i's " fade into the twilight of a
dimmed " i " in :
      " and puerile moving of your arm will "
This pattern of long and poignant and unsharp

" i's " echoes through the poem, and their particularly subtle and beautiful arrangement is mainly responsible for the movement and rhythm of this poem. Nobody is more skilful than Mr. Cummings in producing a subtlety of rhythm and of movement (these are nearly, but not quite, the same thing, since the question of speed or of slowing down comes under the heading of movement) by the means of assonances placed at irregular intervals, and by the means of assonances mingled with dissonances. We find this, again, in the lines :

" [1]will [2]do

more than [3]heroes beautifully in [1]shrill

[4]armour colliding on [3]huge [2]blue horses,

and the poets [2]looked at them, and made verses,

[2]through the sharp [4]light [4]cryingly as the [4]knights

[2]flew."

The dewy sounds in " do," " blue," " flew," and " through," are intermingled with the leaf-sharp, leaf-cool dissonances of " beautifully " and " huge." The vowel-sound in " looked " is dimmer, more shadowy, than that of " looked." Then, in the last line, we have the long " i's " gathered together into one final poignant beauty, balancing, as it were, the whole poem.

Here, then, we have a gifted poet who, in preference to being an exquisite poet on a minor scale, prefers to be an " innovator " of inferior novelties, and here we have an example of the muddle-headed ideas besetting poetry today.